Oragean Modernism: A lost literary movement, 1924-1953, including A.R. Orage, Carl Van Vechten, Djuna Barnes, John Dos Passos, Arna Bontemps, Nathaniel West, Dawn Powell, James Agee, Maxwell Perkins, Zora Neale Hurston, Ralph Ellison, C. Daly King, Angelo Herndon, John O'Hara, Dorothy West, Elinor Wylie, and Marjorie Kinnan Rawlings

By

Jon Woodson

2013

Oragean Modernism: a lost literary movement, 1924-1953

Copyright 2013 Jon Woodson

Cover photo:
Moon Model prepared by Johann Friedrich Julius Schmidt, Germany in 1898. Made of 116 sections of plaster on a framework of wood and metal. Wood floor, Security Guard in uniform in background, stairs leading up to the left. Sign above door "Geology"... Presented to the Field Columbian Museum in 1898 by Lewis Reese of Chicago.

TO

Morgan Woodson

Contents

"[The] world was experiencing one of its periodic outbursts of "utopian longing." The 1920s and 1930s [were] decades wherein man's achievement of perfection appeared to many to be imminent."

—Michael A. Orgozaly, *Waldo Frank, Prophet of Hispanic Regeneration*

"For us, *who are not yet men*, that responsibility is but the weightier by reason of the words, not yet.... Every man must somehow find how he can become genuinely human; and to discover this, he must first find out what 'human' really means."

—C. Daly King, *The Oragean Version*

"Moon's too pretty fuh anybody tuh be sleepin' it away."

—Zora Neale Hurston, *Their Eyes Were Watching God*

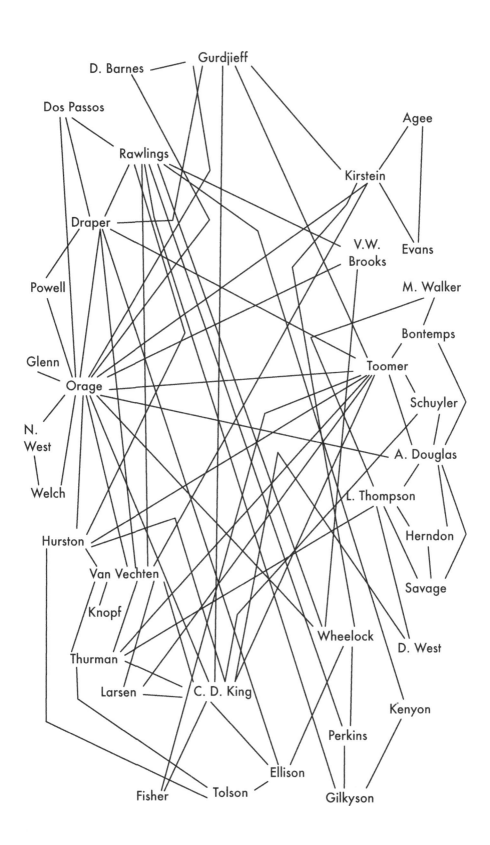

Chapter 1. Oragean Modernism

1. Involution or Evolution: Literary Suprematism and the Struggle to Save the Planet Earth

Oragean Modernism is a lost modernist literary movement; its goal was the salvation of the planet Earth through disseminating works of popular literature with an esoteric content. I have bracketed Oragean Modernism with the dates 1924-1952—the first date corresponding to George Ivanovich Gurdjieff's first visit to America and the second date corresponding to the publication of Ralph Ellison's novel, *Invisible Man.* Ellison's novel won the National Book Award in 1953. Oragean Modernism was a direct result of the introduction into America of the teachings of the modern mystic George Ivanovich Gurdjieff[1]. Arvan Harvat, a highly skeptical critic of the Gurdjieff Work, described the man and his teachings in these terms:

> Gurdjieff can be best described as a blend of operating Theosophist and the protagonist of Neopythagorean/Rosicrucian-Hermetic doctrines in vogue [during] these times (turn of the 19/20th century.)
>
> What the Theosophical movement had been teaching in last two decades of the 19th century, Gurdjieff, armed with his vitalist temper and adventurous spirit tried to achieve in practice. For all the nice talk about India and "Masters", Theosophists remained an influential, but rather impotent debate club. Our hero, Georgi Ivanovitch Gurdjieff, yearned for "the right stuff" of superhuman mastery and actualization of the "miraculous", a pervasive theme during the *fin de siecle.* (Harvat "Gurdjieff, Enneagram, and the Fourth Way")

Recognizing that they lived in increasingly perilous times, many of the sharpest intellects and talents of the 1920s and 1930s enrolled in a covert plan to reverse the destructive course that they felt was leading to inevitable planetary doom. While it may seem to us absurd for a group of writers to plunge into the creation of literary texts in an effort to subvert widespread catastrophe, it was one of the most important aspects of the Oragean Modernist vision that literature was an efficacious means to recruit the number of advanced humans that they required for planetary rescue; if they failed, the literary texts would preserve the esoteric teachings for future generations.

Strictly speaking, the writings published by the Oragean Modernists were not *esoteric*. Occult practices defined activities as being exoteric, mesoteric and esoteric, with all of these categories subsumed under the looser sense of "esoteric": exoteric materials were more or less public, while mesoteric and esoteric materials were only divulged to those who had passed through some form of initiation. The published writings of the Oragean Modernists contained or were formed from the exoteric teachings of the Oragean version of the Gurdjieff Work, also called the Fourth Way. The Oragean Modernist salvation of the Earth was based on what can be thought of as "planetary alchemy," so in their view their activities were not subject to the methods and limits by which in the normal course events are manipulated—wars, revolutions, and technological systems.

The Oragean Modernists believed that the root causes of planetary difficulties were derived from the influence of the Moon. *Gurdjieff: The Key* Concepts summarizes Gurdjieff's teachings about the Moon as follows:

> The Moon is referred to in relation to the outer world, the macrocosm, in terms of the Ray of Creation, and also in relation to man's inner world, the microcosm, where the Moon represents a passive force equated with involution and mechanicality. Man gains liberation from his 'inner moon' through the growth of mental powers and the development of consciousness and will.
>
> In relation to the macrocosm, the Moon is a living being evolving to become a planet. The energy for its growth comes from the Sun and the planets of our solar

system. This energy is collected in a huge accumulator that is formed by organic life on the Earth. Everything living on Earth is food for the Moon. No energy is lost in the universe; on Earth the death of each mineral, plant, animal or man sets free some energy. These 'souls' that go to the Moon may possess some consciousness and memory, but under conditions of mineral life can only be freed after immeasurably long cycles of general planetary evolution. In Christian terms, the Moon is 'outer darkness'. Man as he is cannot free himself from the Moon, which controls all his actions of every kind, including the evil, criminal, self-sacrificing and heroic.

The Moon and Earth are interdependent; the Moon is an electromagnet that 'sucks out the vitality of organic life'. If its action stopped, organic life would crumble to nothing (*Search*:83-6). The Moon is like the weight in a clock, and organic life is like the mechanism brought into motion by that weight. If the weight were removed, the mechanism would stop (*Search*: 95; see also law of reciprocal maintenance / reciprocal feeding).

There are different definitions of the Moon: one as the growing tip of the Ray of Creation, and the other as its dead end. In the first definition, the Ray of Creation from Absolute to Moon is like a growing branch of a tree. If the Moon does not grow the whole Ray of Creation will stop or find a new path for growth (*Search*: 304_6). However, Gurdjieff also said that, in the line from Absolute to Moon, 'the moon is the last point of creation on this line' (*Views*, 1924: 1,96).

Food that satisfies the Moon at one period may not be enough later on, so organic life must evolve to sustain the Moon (*Views*, 1924: 196). 'The moon is man's big enemy'. 'We are like sheep that the Moon feeds and shears. When 'she' is hungry she kills a lot of us. Passive man serves the moon and involution. Inside us we have a moon, and if we knew what our inner moon is and does, we would understand the cosmos (*Views*, 1924: 198). (Wellbeloved 144-45)

Gurdjieff taught that the influence of the Moon upon everything living manifests itself in all that happens on Earth. Man can not tear himself free from the Moon. All his movements and consequently all his actions are controlled by the Moon. Man is a machine, and the mechanical part of our life is subject to the Moon. Thus Oragean Modernist writers applied themselves assiduously to the task of producing and disseminating a specific type of literary work that beneath its entertaining exterior contained a uniform "esoteric" content.

The history of the Oragean Modernist movement is filled with controversies that continue to this day. As this is a brief study, I will point out that there was a crisis in 1931, when Gurdjieff and Orage came into conflict. Since this is an account of the Oragean Modernist side of the conflict, more can be learned from Oragean Modernist sources, the most important being C. Daly King's presentation of Orage's teachings. In *The Oragean Version* King explains that once Orage split with Gurdjieff, the American groups were without a leader:

> In New York, with M. Gurdjieff's departure, matters naturally were left in some confusion. Certain of the former group members arranged to meet for further readings from the Gurdjieff manuscripts and I myself organized a small group, not conducted as previously, but concerned solely with a particular experimental work in connection with that Method which will be formulated in the body of this treatise. The next year, 1932, I published the *Psychology of Consciousness,* a much more detailed, technical and expanded version of the earlier *Beyond Behaviorism.* (King 9)

One of the benefits of studying the novels of the Oragean Modernists is that by combining their accounts, it is possible to arrive at a picture of how the groups carried on after Orage's departure in 1931.

My discovery of Oragean Modernism proceeded though several distinct stages. I want to relate how this discovery came about so that there will be a good understanding of my relationship to the discovery of the movement and of my explication of its literary texts. As a child my interest in poetry was aroused by having been taken to see Carl Sandburg in 1956: Sandburg performed for Negro children at the Library of Congress. There was little poetry in my home, but I did discover selections of Walt Whitman's *Leaves of Grass* in a poetry anthology that had been one of my father's college textbooks, and I read them with great interest. A particularly important point in my development was my discovery of Ezra Pound's *Cantos* while browsing in the public library: I developed a sustained appreciation for Pound's magnum opus though I had little grasp of the deeper significance of the man or the book. In high school I began to become aware of modern literature and to write poetry that imitated e.e. cummings and the Beat poets; this interest was maintained though my college education. Through a fortunate circumstance, in 1969 I was hired to teach at Lincoln University, an HBCU, in the Thirteen College Curriculum Program consortium, where I came directly into contact with African-American literature and with African-American writers for the first time. In 1971 Arthur Davis, one of the consultants to the TCCP, included a poem of mine in *Cavalcade*, a popular African-American literature text book. For the first time I began to experience the literary-political consequences of being black and writing poetry, and I resolved to withdraw from an active pursuit of writing for publication. At the same time, my first visit to the campus bookstore at Lincoln University caused me to take a look at Lincoln University alumnus Melvin B. Tolson's book-length epic poem, *Harlem Gallery*. I was fascinated to see that there was a Poundian poem by an African-American, and right on the spot I resolved to write a dissertation on Tolson, a safe thing to wish for since at the time I had no plan to study for a PhD. As events transpired, it did behoove me to move towards an advanced degree, and when the time came, I did take up the study of Tolson's poetry. While living in Providence, R.I. and studying at Brown University, I had occasion to spend a lot of time in the company of the avant-garde writer and musician, Alan Sondheim. Sondheim was by far the most acquisitive person that I have ever known, and one day he came to my house and deposited a small library of books on the occult. He declared himself the master of their contents and said that he was thus through with them. Though it was probably a poor idea to have done so at the time, as I was engaged in my graduate studies, inspired by Sondheim's comment, I endeavored to read the entire collection of books on the occult. Recovering from this diversion, I got on with my work and began to attack my Tolson project in earnest. Along the way, it became apparent that there was something amiss with Tolson, since his poetry showed outward signs of a significant interest in the occult, though this was not acknowledged by the few critics who at that early stage had published on Tolson. But there were significant tokens of a deep concern with the occult in Tolson's poetry, and before long, I could see that Tolson had drawn deeply on the writings of P.D. Ouspensky in order to shape his poems, and that Tolson was nothing less than a follower of George Ivanovich Gurdjieff. Though I was successful in earning a PhD with my dissertation on Tolson, because of my view of Tolson as an occultist, my findings were summarily dismissed by the critics who began in the late 1970s to publish studies of Tolson. Not wishing to leave things at that point, I began to look into how it was that a black poet who lived in Texas and Indiana could be an occultist. My interest in occultism was a matter of intellectual curiosity. I was never a follower of Gurdjieff or a member of any esoteric group. I am a literary scholar who happened to acquire a general acquaintance with the literature of esotericism—a body of knowledge that few literary scholars come into contact with. As a result of this introduction to the esoteric, I was able to recognize the esoteric contents of the poetry of Melvin B. Tolson.

After many years of research, I was able to publish *To Make a New Race: Gurdjieff, Toomer, and the Harlem Renaissance* (1999). In that study I showed that the entire Harlem Renaissance was penetrated by the influence of the occult. Jean Toomer has been established as having taught the Gurdjieff Work to the Harlem writers, but Toomer's brief association with Harlem has also suggested that the Harlem Renaissance's affiliation with the Gurdjieffians was superficial. This is a complex matter, and it may be cleared up by first stating that in Harlem the Gurdjieff Work was primarily taught by C. Daly King, so that when Toomer moved to Chicago, King continued to teach the Harlem groups; the Harlem followers also studied with other groups in New York and even went to Paris, where Gurdjieff had a permanent school. Secondly, the prominent members of the Harlem Renaissance who were not occultists, like Langston Hughes and Countee Cullen, were unaware of the activities of the Gurdjieffians, and the outsiders continued to publish alongside the esotericists. The famous issue of the literary magazine *Fire!!!* is an example of a Gurdjieffian publication that contained writings by non-esoteric writers and that is not perceived to have any connection to the Oragean Modernists. Carl Van Vechten, who funded the issue of *Fire!!!*, the figure most often given credit for stimulating the Harlem Renaissance movement, was a prominent and active Gurdjieffian. Van Vechten's name appears on the membership list of the New York group of Gurdjieffians that was assembled by Muriel Draper, the Gurdjieff movement's New York secretary and one of Van Vechten's closest associates. It was Van Vechten himself who collected and donated Muriel Draper's papers to the Beinecke Library at Yale University. Van Vechten's centrality in the Harlem Renaissance is undisputed, as urged for example by Emily Bernard in her book *Carl Van Vechten and the Harlem Renaissance* (2012)—though without any hint, while his centrality is being argued, that Van Vechten was an occultist. Thus—through Van Vechten— there is a fundamental and inescapable connection of the Harlem Renaissance to occultism.

For his part, Melvin Tolson had studied at Columbia University in 1932, and his master's thesis was the first scholarly study on the Harlem writers, so Tolson had every opportunity to have been recruited by the Harlem Gurdjieffians. It is by no means a stretch to see that the Harlem writers's pervasive interest in the occult that I had identified through my study of Tolson's poetry was born out by the circumstances of Tolson's experiences, contacts, and productions. Not that these disclosures made any headway, for literary scholarship is a game of follow the leader. The prevailing critical works on Tolson praised him for being a good poet while at the same time lambasting him for being a hapless imitator of high modernism. At best Robert Farnsworth declared Tolson an eccentric, and at worst—for Wilburn Williams Jr. and Michael Berube,—Tolson was a dolt. As my study of the Oragean Modernists is to be a brief account, I will direct those who want to know more about Tolson's reception to refer the works of those scholars mentioned above.

I failed to convince many scholars of the truth of what I was saying about Tolson's occultism being derived from the wider occult influence of the Harlem Renaissance. I continued my research, and as I looked further into the texts written in the 1930s, I began to see that rather than the Oragean Modernist movement being confined to the figures that I had been limited to studying, it was a much larger movement. I first added other African-Americans to the list of occultists—Dorothy West, Arna Bontemps, Georgia Douglas Johnson, Gwendolyn Bennett, and Ralph Ellison. I also saw that C. Daly King had played a larger role than I had at first understood, even instructing the Harlem group. I also had the good sense to read the novels by Carl Van Vechten, works universally ignored, and found them to be in every way contiguous with the novels of the Harlem Renaissance occultists: even *Nigger Heaven*, Carl Van Vechten's controversial novel that still plays a role in evaluations of the Harlem Renaissance, is itself an esoteric text.

Like the Harlem Renaissance texts that I discuss in *To Make a New Race*, Van Vechten's novel recapitulates Gurdjieff's body of teachings (the Gurdjieff Work) and is written in the alchemical code called the *cabala*—about which considerably more will be said below. There is an extraordinary passage towards the conclusion of *Nigger Heaven* in which it is explained that there is a "code" used in a particular Harlem restaurant: "That's part of the code used here, she explained" (241). It is related that when patrons who appear to be wealthy arrive, they are greeted as "Mr.

Gunnion" (241). This rude and intolerable handling of patrons could not have taken place in a successful restaurant, and it is clearly a "lawful inexactitude" meant to indicate that there is esoteric content in the passage. Since Gurdjieff was commonly referred to by his followers as "Mr. G.," and since the goal of his teaching was to produce unity in the self ("one 'I'"), the name "Mr. Gunnion" (Mr. G.—union) is an indication of Van Vechten's interest in the teachings of George Ivanovich Gurdjieff. The riddle of Van Vechten's code may not be transparent, but it is easily solved by anyone with the proper background.

Finally, the breakthrough came wherein I realized the scope of Oragean Modernism. A scholar who had read my book *To Make a New Race* wrote to me and told me that James Agee's book, *Let Us Now Praise Famous Men*, was the same sort of Gurdjieffian literary construction that I had been writing about in connection with Tolson, Hurston, Larsen, Fisher, Thurman, and Schuyler. This was a surprise to me, since originally I had contacted the scholar about some of Zora Neale Hurston's early writings, so it was unexpected to hear about Agee (from what turned out to be an Agee expert) in the returning message. Following up on this lead, I began to widen the Oragean Modernist circle by including the white authors who were the literary followers of A.R. Orage. I managed to discover who belonged to the school by following chains of associations; essentially, it was a matter of taking literary gossip seriously.

While it is now possible to describe the esoteric content of the Oragean Modernist's literary works and to describe some details of their planned historical intervention, some aspects of the Oragean Modernist project still remain unknowns. A chief unknown is the means by which this new literary genre was conceived and modeled: it is possible that there is in existence the ur-novel of the Oragean Modernists, but to date it has not been discovered. On the other hand, there may not be such an ur-novel at all. In any case, it is apparent that at times the effect of the esoteric satirical novels on those personages who were sensitive to literature was to arouse suspicions about the texts and their authors. In a letter dated July 18th, 1925 here is what Ellen Glasgow had to say about Van

Vechten's esoteric novel *Firecrackers*. The protagonist of *Firecrackers* is a thinly disguised Jean Toomer. The novel also mentions Gurdjieff and Ouspensky by name, as well as containing passages concerning mysticism:

Dear Carl,

Firecrackers reached Richmond after I had left, and making a short stay there in my absence, caught up with me brilliantly a few days ago. I took the Federal Express at Washington and came straight up that same night without stopping in New York. That is why you did not hear from me. Yesterday afternoon and last night I spent with your [indecipherable] and terrible book. After I once began it, I was oblivious of everything around me until I was finished. The first chapter is amazingly clear. I felt the fascination of the [indecipherable] from the moment he entered until the end of the book. The whole thing is diabolically clever, and so profoundly depressing as any "realistic" novel ever written. I have, too, after reading it with much interest and pleasure the curious feeling that this is a trackless wilderness under you, a desert-hell, not garden but jungle—that I do not know and have never even had a glimpse of. *Someday I must talk to you about this, and try to discover how many Carls there are in reality, and if my Carl has any actual relation to the innumerable other Carls.* But you have an extraordinary power of [indecipherable] terror. Not since Balzac has there been a more terrible ending scene than the ending of the Countess.

I hope you are having a pleasant working summer. Up here in this retreat I am idling away July and August. I can't work, but play… every morning and …afternoon.

In September I hope to be in New York for a few days, &
if you are there, I shall look forward to seeing you and
talking more about your book.

Sincerely yours,
Ellen Glasgow
(Glasgow 1958, 78-9) (Hocutt 12-13; emphasis added)

A further difficulty in discovering more about Oragean
Modernism arises with the difficulty of extracting information
from the novels of the Oragean Modernists, for the style in which
the information is delivered often puts the critic at the risk of
reading things into the texts that may not have been intended. In
Dawn Powell's novel *Turn, Magic Wheel* she seems to be pointing
to exactly the sort of ur-novel that was the chief means of
dissemination for the Gurdjieff Work by the Oragean Modernists—
the satirical novel: "…we can cite a dozen famous authors' wives
whose portraits conform to this satiric outline" (103). The
descriptive phrase "conform to this satiric outline" seems to point
to the similarities in the inclusion of esoteric features among the
novels by Carl Van Vechten, Dawn Powell, Djuna Barnes and
many others. While Powell may well be pointing the reader to the
existence of a body of esoteric novels, it is difficult to take this
instance as her definitive confirmation of such an esoteric "satiric
outline"—though one certainly suspects that this was Dawn
Powell's intention.

The Oragean Modernists subscribed to an unfamiliar ethos.
As they saw their role on the planet, it was a given that they were
above all supermen, and as such they may not have seen fit to
reveal any more of their arrangements than they felt obliged to.
Secrecy was important to the Oragean Modernists. While I have
been searching through their texts for an account of their
organization, it is possible that no such account was ever set down.
It is also possible that the somewhat vague mode of their esoteric
writing has covered over this account too well, and that it has been
placed in plain sight but not yet been properly interpreted. One of
the factors that I have had to deal with in this study is that all of the

Oragean Modernist writers went about encoding their writings in variations on the phonetic *cabala*, so it is difficult to carry over what one has learned from one writer to another writer. For instance, there is a very interesting passage in Zora Neale Hurston's novel *Seraph on the Suwanee* that describes fishing that may well have been intended to reveal a great deal about the organizational history of the Oragean Modernists, but the passage is too ambiguous to allow anything definitive to be said: this passage will be discussed below. Since the esoteric content of Oragean Modernist texts has been invisible to most readers all along, it should hardly be surprising if specific components of their project have not been assessed. My *Oragean Modernism* is but a preliminary study of this topic, and while I have made what I consider a great deal of progress in the understanding of this literary movement, I by no means have the right to claim that in this study I am presenting the entire picture of the Oragean Modernist movement.

The two generative figures from which the Gurdjieff Work sprang, George Ivanovich Gurdjieff and P.D. Ouspensky, were both prolific writers. Gurdjieff's writings were cast as works of fiction, the most important work being *Beelzebub's Tales*, a 1,000 page work of science fiction that narrated the adventures of an eternal supernatural being who traveled the universe in a space ship. Ouspensky wrote treatises in varying styles of accessibility, though he also produced a work of fiction, a novel about eternal recurrence, *The Strange Life of Ivan Osokin*—the source text for a popular film, *Groundhog Day* (1993). It is useful to consider the connection between the Gurdjieff Work and science fiction at this initial point in discussing Oragean Modernism in order to point out that the planetary scale of the concerns of Orage's followers was fundamental to their ideology. In fact, the planetary scale of the relationship between the Earth and the Moon that was the focus of the Oragean Modernists represents more a shrinkage of scale than an expansion, since vast spans of time and space were covered in Ouspensky's discussions of the seven cosmoses in Gurdjieff's metaphysics:

Protocosmos -- the first cosmos (the Absolute, "1")

Ayocosmos or Megalocosmos -- the holy cosmos (all worlds, "3")

Macrocosmos -- the large cosmos (Milky Way, "6")

Deuterocosmos -- the second cosmos (the Sun, the solar system, "12")

Mesocosmos -- the middle cosmos (all planets, "24")

Tritocosmos -- the third cosmos (man, "48")

Microcosmos -- the small cosmos (atom)

(*In Search of the Miraculous* 205)

Ouspensky presented the relationships between these "cosmoses" in another chart:

Orders of the "world"

1st order world is affected by 1 force -- the single, independent will of the Absolute

2nd order world is affected by 3 forces (all the galaxies)

3rd order world is affected by 6 forces (Milky Way) - (3 [from 2nd] + 3 new forces)

4th order world is affected by 12 forces (our Sun) - (3 [from 2nd] + 6 [from 3rd] + 3 new forces)

5th order world is affected by 24 forces (planets in our solar system) - (3 [from 2nd] + 6 [from 3rd] + 12 [from 4th] + 3 new forces)

6th order world is affected by 48 forces (Earth) - (3 [from 2nd] + 6 [from 3rd] + 12 [from 4th] + 24 [from 5th] + 3 new forces)

7th order world is affect by 96 forces (Moon) - (3 [2nd] + 6 [3rd] + 12 [4th] + 24 [from 5th] + 48 [from 6th] + 3 new forces)

(*In Search of the Miraculous* 80)

These vast scales were absorbed by the writers who were influenced by the published writings of Gurdjieff and Ouspensky, while the Oragean Modernists who were actually enrolled directly in Gurdjieff's esoteric school tended to concentrate on the Earth and the Moon. Frank Herbert, one of the most important contemporary science fiction writers, was heavily influenced by Ouspensky's books, and thus *Dune* and the *Dune* cycle, breakthrough science fiction texts, relate the story of intergalactic empires across thousands of years of history. According to Gurdjieff, each cosmos is a living being which lives, breathes, thinks, feels, is born, and dies; following up on this idea, Herbert wrote *Whipping Star* in which an "alien" intelligence is a star—in Gurdjieff's terms a fourth order world. Steering closer to the concerns of the Oragean Modernists, Frank Herbert centered *Dune* on the idea of the superman: in the Gurdjieffian system there are seven types of man:

Man #1 is the man of the physical body.

Man #2 is the emotional man.

Man #3 is the man of reason whose knowledge is based on scholastics.

Man #4 is a man who has ideals.

Man #5 is a man who has reached unity and has already been crystallized.

Man #6 is very close to the ideal man, but some of his properties have not yet become permanent.

Man #7 is the man who had reached the full development possible to man.

For Gurdjieff, Man 5, 6, and 7 are "artificial," for they are the products of esoteric schools of self-development; such men do not exist in nature. In Frank Herbert's science fiction novel, *Dune*, this *spiritual* mode of advanced development has been replaced by a millennia-old *genetic* program operated by the *Bene Gesserit*, an order of women with a goal of producing a male *Bene Gesserit*, called the *Kwisatz Haderach*. The nature of the superman has been switched from spiritual to genetic. The *Kwisatz Haderach* would be capable of accessing all ancestral memories and could possess "organic mental powers" that can "bridge space and time." Frank Herbert's *Kwisatz Haderach* is equivalent to Gurdjieff's Man #7.

As we shall see, the politics of the Gurdjieff and the Oragean Modernist movements were centered on the divisive issue of the priority that each gave to the production of Man #7 as opposed to other concerns.

The science fiction cycle authored by Doris Lessing draws heavily from Gurdjieff —rather than from Ouspensky—in depicting an interplanetary reality, and in *The Making of a Representative for Planet 8* echoes even Gurdjieff's outré literary style. Lessing's treatment of science fiction is impure, and in *Briefing for a Descent into Hell* she drew heavily on Ouspensky and distinguished that novel from the *Canopus in Argos* series by designating *Briefing* as belonging to the genre of "inner 'space fiction'"(Fishburn 48). Gurdjieff's Beelzebub is an exile who lives on Mars, from which vantage he observes life on the planet Earth: Gurdjieff's novel describes Beelzebub's six visits to Earth in order to purge the human race of such excesses as animal sacrifice and war. Lessing's novels are situated in a realist mode, and the interventions in human history are made by agents of advanced civilizations with the technological capacity to cross intergalactic spaces.

Unlike these science fiction writers who borrowed from Gurdjieff and Ouspensky, the Oragean Modernists were individuals who in many cases had met Gurdjieff in America or who had gone to France and studied with him. Other Oragean Modernists only had contact with A.R. Orage. The politics of the Gurdjieff movement are somewhat complex, but it will suffice to say that there was a split between G.I. Gurdjieff and A.R. Orage and that some members of the American school maintained loyalty to Gurdjieff and some to Orage. In many Oragean Modernist texts Gurdjieff is portrayed as a villain. One of the complexities of Gurdjieffian-Oragean politics is that it is not possible to tell by outward signs who was loyal to either teacher: for example, Djuna Barnes does not seem to have been a follower of either teacher, though she was intermittently and serially romantically affiliated with the women belonging to the group of Gurdjieff's followers who lived in Paris and were called The Rope; however, a close reading of her novel *Nightwood* makes it evident that she was a follower of Orage, for like many of the Oragean Modernists she casts Gurdjieff as a villain in her novel.

In so far as this study is concerned, the chief difference between the Gurdjieffians and the Oragean Modernists is that the European and American followers of Gurdjieff who studied at his school in France simply did not write expressive literature as part of their program; many Gurdjieffians wrote and published "unauthorized" descriptions of their studies with Gurdjieff. This is not to say that there is no Gurdjieffian creative writing, for some of Gurdjieff's direct followers did produce expressive esoteric literary texts—the writings of the surrealist poet and novelist Rene Daumal being one example of this tendency. But Gurdjieff did not encourage his students to write, and Daumal's writings have no official standing in relation to the Gurdjieff Work. In contrast to Gurdjieff's dismissal of the writings of his students, Orage routinely organized creative writing groups, and while he lived in New York, a great deal of Orage's time and energy went into the teaching of writing. Secrecy prevailed among the Oragean Modernists, so that in the most detailed account of Orage's eight years in New York, Louise Welch's *Orage with Gurdjieff in America* (1982), the list of writers does not correspond very well with the list of writers that I have compiled from my own research. Nothing in Welch's account suggests an overall plan for the writings of the Oragean Modernist group, and instead there are mentions of "trying to place [texts] in the objective order demanded by their depth" and the "perception of illness through style" (63). Nor does Welch's presentation make evident much that we would like to know about what went on in those meetings, for there is a great departure between the contents of the writings by the Oragean Modernists and what we have been given to expect from Welch's account.

Oragean Modernist writing was never allowed the expansiveness of Gurdjieffian cosmic science fiction, and in fact there is only one published work of Oragean Modernist science fiction, George Schuyler's *Black No More*. Schuyler tells a story in which a scientist finds a way to turn African-Americans into white people, hardly a cosmic exercise. In the Oragean Modernist canon it is the satirical novel that predominates. Other genres of fiction include historical novels (Bontemps, Gilkyson, Wylie, Lincoln

Kirstein, and Margaret Walker), regional novels (Rawlings, Hurston), and detective stories (C. Daly King, Rudolph Fisher). Some Oragean Modernist writers published short stories in newspapers and periodicals. In addition there are a few esoteric nonfiction works of anthropology, social criticism, and psychology. There were also volumes of poetry, and there were some dramatic works. The writings that were not extended works of fiction presented the authors with challenges in the handling of the hidden esoteric content: in *A Gallery of Harlem Portraits* Melvin Tolson used odd names for the characters in his spare poems that imitated *The Spoon River Anthology*, so that his table of contents carries a Gurdjieffian subtext. Zora Neal Hurston entitled one of her plays *Cold Keener*, a phrase meaningless to contemporary Hurston scholars who are tone deaf to the simplicity of a phonetic trickery that simply says "code key."

2. A.R. Orage and Esoteric Realism

Arthur Richard Orage does not figure very much in American literary history. Orage is entirely absent from *Terrible Honesty: Mongrel Manhattan in the 1920's*, Ann Douglas's "biography" of New York in the 1920s. He is absent from *The Encyclopedia of the Harlem Renaissance* (Finkleman, Wintz). Nor does Orage make an appearance in Jack Selzer's *Kenneth Burke in Greenwich Village: Conversing with the Moderns, 1915—1931*, a more detailed study of the circles that were contemporaneous with and that overlapped the Oragean Modernists. Following the methodology of American Studies scholars, Selzer's study makes no mention of the occult, choosing to see all of the activities of the modernists as "literary nationalism" (31-39). In all of this I am reminded of the treatment of history in George Orwell's *1984*. You will recall that the protagonist, Winston Smith works as a clerk in the Records Department of the Ministry of Truth, where his job is to rewrite historical documents so they match the constantly changing current party line. This involves revising newspaper articles and doctoring photographs—mostly to remove "unpersons," people who have fallen foul of the party. Thus I will begin this study by pointing out that in the discourses of American literary history, American Studies, and cultural studies, A.R. Orage is an "unperson." The one exception to this leaning that I have found is the American Studies scholar Robert Crunden. In *Body and Soul: The Making of American Modernism* Crunden lamented the "misleading" neglect of "the occult" by scholars (344). Crunden stated that "The influence of G.I. Gurdjieff, P.D. Ouspensky, and A.R. Orage in America or among Americans abroad was substantial, touching many briefly, destroying promising careers, and energizing a few for life" (344). Crunden did no research of his own and depended on Louise Welch and Langston Hughes for his account of the Gurdjieff Work. Welch kept silent about the important things, and Hughes was not in the Work, so what he had to say was untrustworthy: realizing the paucity of his information, Crunden himself admits that he has no real idea of what the folllowers of Gurdjieff were doing. Nevertheless, it is interesting to see that despite these limitations Crunden argued in favor of the centrality of the occult in the formation of American Modernism.

I have had to supply the cognomen "Oragean Modernism" to fill the void in the present narrative of American literature. Orage directed creative writing seminars that included many important and influential figures of that time and place. What came out of those seminars was a literary movement on a par with the recognized movements of the period—imagism, dada, Futurism, and its near contemporary, Surrealism—a movement that produced a host of texts, some canonical. Unlike these public avant-gardes, Oragean Modernism did not openly disseminate a manifesto. The inner constructs of Oragean Modernism are unknown.

The combined endorsements of P.D. Ouspensky and A.R. Orage attracted a wide following to the Gurdjieff Work. What cannot be established is which of those persons who attended Gurdjieff's performances and Orage's lectures became permanently affiliated with Oragean Modernism. There is little external evidence to aid the compilation of a list of Oragean Modernists. What I have done is to examine the accounts of the initial attendees and then examined their writings for esoteric contents. One of the longest lists of potential Oragean Modernists was supplied by Paul Beekman Taylor:

In November, Orage had a large group before him to address. It grew over time to include the short-story writer Israel Solon, the literary critic Van Wyck Brooks, businessmen Stanley Speidelberg and Sherman Manchester, detective-novel writer and psychologist C. Daly King, music reviewer Muriel Draper, actor Edwin Wolfe, architects Claude Bragdon and Hugh Ferris, five-and-dime heiress Blanche Rossette Grant, writer T. S. Matthews and his sister Peggy (son and daughter of the Bishop of New Jersey), writer Lawrence S. Hare and his art-patron wife Betty Meredith Sage, poets Melville Cane and Edna Kenton, painter Boardman Robinson, Claire Mann, writer-publisher C. Stanley Nott, writers Waldo Frank, Carl Bechhofer Roberts, Gorham Munson, and Schuyler Jackson, editor of *Modern School* Carl Zigrosser, editor of *The New Republic* Herbert Croly, literary editor of the *New York World* John Cosgrove O'Hara, concert pianists Carol Robinson and Rosemary Lillard, Doctor Louis Berman (the instigator of Gurdjieff's "The Material Question" at the conclusion of *Meetings with Remarkable Men*), Helen Westley of the Theater Guild, the historical novelist Mary Johnston, mathematician and short-story writer John Riordan, editor of *The Little Review* Jane Heap, and, of course, the author of *Cane*, Jean Toomer. These were joined by occasional visitors, including novelist Zona Gale, poet Hart Crane, editor of the *Double-Dealer* John McLure, poetess Mavis McIntosh, and, most significantly, patroness of the arts Mabel Dodge Luhan. Over the next few years, regulars included the fashion editor and lovelorn columnist Louise Michel [Louise Welch], the painter and writer Walter Inglis Anderson, impresario Lincoln Kirstein, and Swiss consul in New York Robert Schwartzenbach and his wife Marguerite, Katie Powys dragged her brother Llewelyn to hear Orage, and before long, John Cowper Powys, who had regretted Orage's quitting *The New Age* became interested in Orage's new ideas. Before the end of the year, as many as two hundred people had joined his groups, the fee for which was ten dollars per month. Besides these, there were any number of guests, curious to see and hear Orage. Zona Gale's protégée, the novelist Margery Latimer—later married to Jean Toomer—attended at least one Meeting with Kenneth Fearing that winter. The main group met that fall in Jane Heap's and Margaret Anderson's apartment at 24 East 11 th Street. (Taylor 93-4)

From Taylor's account it is clear that persons from many fields were attracted to Orage. This study closely tracks only the fiction writers and a few artists and publishers. The writers of long prose works are the only source of internal information about the Oragean Modernists. The artists included in this study either supply additional internal information in their works of art or through their specific affiliations. The publishers discussed in this study underscore the degree to which the Oragean Modernists were able to carry out their program through infiltrating important organizations. Given the limitations on what can be known, the following list of the writers that this study centers on cannot claim to be complete. I have called the second division the "Greenwich Village Group" for convenience, for all of the members did not live in Greenwich Village.

Oragean Modernist Novelists and Short-Story Writers

The Harlem Group

Arna Bontemps — *God Sends Sunday* (1931), *Black Thunder* (1936)
Rudolph Fisher — *The Walls of Jericho* (1928), *The Conjure-Man Dies* (1932)
Langston Hughes — *Not Without Laughter* (1930)

Zora Neale Hurston — *Jonah's Gourd Vine* (1934),*Their Eyes Were Watching God* (1937),*Seraph on the Suwanee* (1938)

Nella Larsen — *Quicksand* (1928), *Passing* (1929)

Richard Bruce Nugent — *Beyond Where the Stars Stood Still* (1945), *Gentleman Jigger* (1928-33,2008)

George Schuyler — *Black No More* (1931), *Slaves Today* (1931)

Wallace Thurman — *The Blacker the Berry* (1929),*Infants of the Spring* (1932), *Interne* (1932)

Melvin B. Tolson—*Harlem Gallery* (1965) [I am including this long poem as being a "novelization" after Bakhtin: "[T]he *novelization* of other genres does not *imply their* subjection to an alien generic canon. Novelization implies the liberation from all that serves as a brake on their unique development." (McKeon 318)]

Carl Van Vechten — *Nigger Heaven* (1926)

Walter White — *The Fire in the Flint* (1924), *Flight* (1926)

"Greenwich Village Group"

James Agee—1941 *Let Us Now Praise Famous Men: Three Tenant Families* , Houghton Mifflin

Djuna Barnes—*Nightwood* (1936)

John Dos Passos—*U.S.A.* (1938). Three-volume set includes *The 42nd Parallel*, (1930), *Nineteen Nineteen,* (1932)*The Big Money* (1936)

Ralph Ellison—*Invisible Man* (Random House, 1952).

Walter Gilkyson—*The Lost Adventurer* (1927)

Isa Glenn—*East of Eden* (1932)

John O'Hara—*Appointment in Samarra* (1934)

Angelo Herndon—*Let Me Live* (1937)

Bernice Lesbia Kenyon—"The Doll." *Harper's Magazine.* November 1936.

Dawn Powell—1936. *Turn, Magic Wheel* New York: Farrar & Rinehart. 1938. *The Happy Island* New York: Farrar & Rinehart. 1940.*Angels on Toast* New York: Charles Scribner's Sons. Reprinted in 1956 as *A Man's Affair.* New York: Fawcett. 1942.*A Time to Be Born* New York: Charles Scribner's Sons. 1944. *My*

Home Is Far Away New York: Charles Scribner's Sons. 1948.*The Locusts Have No King* New York: Charles Scribner's Sons.
Marjorie Kinnan Rawlings—1933 *South Moon Under*, 1935 *Golden Apples*, 1938*The Yearling*
Nathaniel West—*Miss Lonelyhearts* (1933)
Elinor Wylie—*Mr. Hodge & Mr. Hazard.* New York. Knopf, 1928. London: Heinemann, 1928. Chicago: Academy, 1984.

In the absence of any outside recognition of the existence of Oragean Modernism, many of its texts are poorly understood, James Agee's *Let Us Now Praise Famous Men* and Djuna Barnes's *Nightwood* being good examples of problematic Oragean Modernist texts. Other texts that belong to the movement are understood by literary critics to be the products of isolated and marginal writers who seem eccentric or difficult, such as Dawn Powell, Ralph Ellison, Carl Van Vechten,—and Melvin B. Tolson. Largely because of the theory-driven crises (the replacement of research-based scholarship with poststructuralist literary theories) that have enveloped literary studies for the last sixty years, there has been little opportunity to address texts in comprehensively useful ways, so that many flawed studies that are crippled by unacknowledged critical and theoretical orthodoxies have been presented as being definitive, when in reality they are hallucinations.

In 1922 A.R. Orage followed Gurdjieff to France and remained at the Institute for the Harmonious Development of Man until the last weeks of 1923. By January 2 of 1924, Orage was in New York laying plans for Gurdjieff and his troupe to visit New York later in the month. Gurdjieff and company arrived on January 13, 1924. The troupe performed on February 2, and Jean Toomer described Gurdjieff as being "like a monk in a tuxedo" (Taylor 2001, 46). Largely through the influence of Orage, Gurdjieff's visit to the United States was successful in attracting a wide following, many of whom followed Gurdjieff to France to study at his Institute for the Harmonious Development of Man. After talking at length with Orage, Jean Toomer decided that he, too, would go to see Gurdjieff in France (Taylor 2001, 62). On arriving at the

Prieuré, Gurdjieff's estate outside of Paris, Toomer discovered that Gurdjieff had been badly injured in an automobile accident, had closed the Institute, and that he was not wanted. Toomer overcame these initial objections but soon went back to the United States to study with Orage; later he returned to Paris to assist in the editing of Gurdjieff's huge epic,*Beelzebub's Tales.*

Toomer's strongest connection to esotericism was to his teacher, G. I. Gurdjieff: Toomer patterned himself on Gurdjieff, imitating his mannerisms, his many idiosyncrasies of speech, and incorporating Gurdjieff's literary inventions into his own writings, to the point of plagiarizing episodes from *Beelzebub's Tales* in his unpublished novels "Transatlantic" and "The Gallonwerps." Jean Toomer's attachment to Gurdjieff is important to acknowledge and to evaluate, as it was not the pattern for what followed in the Harlem group. Gurdjieff headed a rather large enterprise that he was determined to continue to expand. In order to draw more money to himself, he in effect franchised Orage, and then Toomer, to found chapters of his Institute, which were then expected to funnel large sums of money back to Paris. Orage sent Toomer from the Greenwich Village headquarters of the New York chapter up to Harlem to organize an African American group. This expansion was a training course that allowed Toomer to establish himself as a teacher of the first (exoteric) level of the Gurdjieff Work (or Fourth Way). Toomer was not in Harlem on his own, but was often accompanied by Orage or another advanced figure, the academically trained psychologist, C. Daly King. It is difficult to determine to what extent Toomer independently led the Gurdjieff meetings in Harlem, given that the Harlem members were as devoted to Orage and even to King as they were to Jean Toomer; the members of the Harlem group must have had substantial and intense contact with Orage and King. Once Toomer successfully recruited and established a Gurdjieff group in Harlem, he was sent to Chicago in November of 1926, where he had his own groups,[2] and C. Daly King continued to direct the Harlem Gurdjieff group. Toomer's Chicago groups were not made up of African Americans, but included well-to-do businessmen, intellectuals, and writers from the Gold Coast section of Chicago (Kerman 1987, 170).

Jean Toomer's contribution to Orage's Greenwich Village groups was impressionistically presented in Carl Van Vechten's novel, *Firecrackers* (1925), in which the gymnast, Gunnar O'Grady, is partly based on Jean Toomer who had studied physical training in college and later taught gymnastics (Kerman 1987, 127). The name Gunnar O'Grady is a phonetically coded composite of **G**eorge **I**van**o**vich **G**urdjieff (G.I.G. / G.O.G.), and **A**. **R**. **Or**age (Gunn-**AR O**'**G**rady). Even though there are realistic aspects to Van Vechten's novel, it is a complex work, combining elements of the comic novel with underlying esoteric themes. The *esoteric realism* that Van Vechten pioneered in his novels was the model for most of the fiction written by those of Orage's Harlem followers who were novelists—Nella Larsen, Zora Neale Hurston, Wallace Thurman, Rudolph Fisher, George Schuyler, Bruce Nugent, Arna Bontemps, and Dorothy West. Esoteric realism was an allusive, coded, heteroglossic style that departed in several distinguishing ways from the avant-garde, fourth dimensional fiction[3] written by Gertrude Stein and Jean Toomer. The black esoteric realists who followed A. R. Orage created many of the most significant texts associated with the Harlem Renaissance. *Without the propelling and sustaining influence of esotericism, the Harlem movement would have been bereft of most of its most characteristic and most highly acclaimed literary achievements .*

An argument can be made that modernism in its quest for liberation, power, and individuality was in the final analysis the pursuit of the superman. Like A.R. Orage, Jean Toomer was infused with the superman doctrine, though in Toomer's case it was gained through its expression in the Theosophical books by H.P. Blavatsky that he had read on his own. Once Toomer joined the New York "art as vision group" (Waldo Frank, Gorham Munson, Hart Crane, Margaret Naumburg, and Kenneth Burke)—a group based on P.D. Ouspensky's *Tertium Organum*— in the early 1920s, he was actively engaged in the attainment of cosmic consciousness, the prerequisite for being a superman. If Ouspensky's *Tertium Organum* had initiated the esoteric quest for the superman under Modernism, Ouspensky had himself brought about the next phase of esotericism by bringing Gurdjieff to attention. And it was Gurdjieff's claim that he possessed exactly those esoteric materials required to transform individuals into supermen, and that the form of those materials in his possession was exactly suitable for the spiritual development of modern persons in the most efficient manner.

Though the Gurdjieff Work was heavily dependent on aspects of Theosophy, it departed from Theosophical teachings about the relationship between the role of the followers and "those who know"—as the Gurdjieffians called the conscious circle of humanity. In Theosophy the conscious circle was a group of enlightened spiritual beings who secretly directed the world, hidden and unapproachable masters who sent down the teachings from afar through their intermediaries. But Orage disseminated teachings that admitted the initiates themselves to the inner circle of humanity. Ouspensky stated that "Two hundred conscious people, if they existed and if they find it necessary and legitimate, could change the whole of life on the earth. But either there are not enough of them, or they do not want to, or perhaps the time has not come, or perhaps other people are sleeping too soundly" (Ouspensky *In Search of the Miraculous* 310). The central tenet of Oragean Modernism was that the time had come for the creation of the two hundred conscious people required to redirect life on earth:

> Some crises can be truly desperate, of such a nature that their final outcome for mankind on this planet remains in genuine doubt even for the Schools. At such times it is said that the Hidden Learning is disclosed, much as one might hurl lifebelts indiscriminately into the sea among the struggling fugitives from a sinking ship. *Sauve qui peut.* At such times a rigorous selection is no longer possible; some lifebelt may be caught and used, out of many failures there may be a few successes when successes are most terribly needed. It is just this sort of period which we have now encountered in the history of mankind upon this planet. That is the answer given in

this Version to those who ask why such information is available at this time in this way. (King 37)

Orage rejected the disillusionment that was at times a feature of Modernism, and he aroused his followers to a fever pitch of optimistic super-effort, so that they wrote in an atmosphere of tremendous excitement and commitment: Orage embraced the Nietzschean side of the Work, where Gurdjieff had said, "Only super-efforts count . . .it is better to die making efforts than to live in sleep"(Ouspensky 232). Even though the Oragean esotericists esteemed themselves the only hope for the planet, even they were nothing more than *potentialities*[4] and had to work furiously to overcome their negative attributes. The volume of writing produced by the Oragean Modernists is astonishing, and such consistent literary fertility demonstrates their commitment to the making of super-efforts.

Gurdjieff taught that there were seven types of man: Ouspensky stated that "[Y]ou suppose all men are on the same level, but in reality, one man can be more different from another than a sheep is from a cabbage. There are seven different categories of men." [5] (Bennett 52-3). The Theosophical novelist Bulwyer Lytton had addressed some of these themes in his novel *Zanoni*, where the magus Mejnour seeks "to create a 'mighty and numerous race' of superhuman occult adepts, even if this necessitates the sacrifice of thousands of aspirants for the sake of a single success" (Gibbons 107). Both Orage and Toomer were obsessed with the idea of the superman long before they encountered Gurdjieff. Orage had been responsible for spreading the superman doctrine through his British journal, *The New Age*. In *Nietzsche in Outline and Aphorism* (1907), Orage advocated the rule of the superman as beings capable of *creativity*: "only peculiarly endowed peoples and individuals are capable of creating, that is, lending to things new and high values" (Stone 75). Nietzsche is usually thought of as a philosopher, but Orage classed him an occultist: "it is probable . . . that new faculties, new modes of consciousness, will be needed, as the mystics have always declared; and that the differencing element of man and Superman will be the possession of these" (Gibbons 107). This doctrine made its way to the center of thought in New York, so that when Wallace Thurman emphasizes the need for "creativity" in *Infants of the Spring* (19,118, 254), we can recognize its Nietzschean context.

The only internal historic account of the Harlem Oragean Modernists was Melvin B. Tolson's Master's thesis, *The Harlem Group of Negro Writers* (1940). The thesis was not a detailed account, and far more useful information can be extracted from his allusive epic poem, *Harlem Gallery*. The record of the efforts of the African American Oragean Modernists mainly consists of published works of imaginative literature—novels, long poems, plays, and lyric poems. The practice of Orage's other groups was much different, particularly in that some of them published accounts of their group work or disseminated their informal notes. Like the Harlem Oragean Modernists, the other Oragean Modernist groups published coded novels of esoteric realism and portrayed Gurdjieff in unflattering ways.[6] Orage kept before all of his groups the important distinction between texts that are subjective-accidental and texts that are "objective." Much of what the Oragean Modernists hoped to accomplish was to have been carried out through their "objective" texts.

The models for the coded novels of the Oragean Modernists were Carl Van Vechten's comic satires. Prior to and during the Harlem Renaissance (1922-1930), Carl Van Vechten published eight best-selling novels. Some of Van Vechten's works are coded and contain esoteric doctrines, with ideas from Ouspensky's pre-Gurdjieff writings in the early novels and Gurdjieffian ideas in the later novels. It is important to note that *Van Vechten's occultism and his use of code has previously eluded literary critics and scholars.* Van Vechten's novels are now generally dismissed as being quaint and mannered, except for *Nigger Heaven.* The latter novel is usually discussed in harsh terms for its supposed exploitation of exotic primitivism (or essentialism) and for its supposed racial stereotypes. For these reasons, Van Vechten's *Nigger Heaven* is unquestionably and uniquely notorious for its supposedly negative influence on the Harlem writers. The Harlem group of writers was devoted to Van Vechten, a fact that receives problematic assessments in scholarly accounts of the Harlem Renaissance. One of the only exceptions to the use of comic novel of satire by the Harlem Oragean Modernists was Rudolph Fisher's detective novel, *The Conjure Man Dies* (1932): writing alongside of the Harlem writers, C. Daly King, inventor of the "sealed room" mystery sub-genre, published mystery novels in the 1930s that were, similarly, coded *legominisms* (transmissions of esoteric knowledge). Rudolph Fisher was the only Harlem novelist to adopt King's sub-genre, publishing a "sealed room" detective novel, *The Conjure-Man Dies* (1932). Despite the exploration of the detective genre, however, Fisher departed from King's style and worked in a comic mode that was close to what the other Harlem writers (and Van Vechten) were doing. Fisher's novel is replete with anomalies ("lawful inexactitudes"—indications to the reader to pay attention: women dressed as men, wrong spellings, mis-numbered lists, words that do not exist) and violates the conventions of the detective genre: for instance, the detective does not solve the case, which is solved by two inept clowns.[7] Nella Larsen, Zora Neale Hurston, Wallace Thurman, Rudolph Fisher, George Schuyler, and Dorothy West published novels of comic satire, closely adhering to Carl Van Vechten's esoteric realism. Variations from this formula were Hurston's experiments with new forms, basing some of her work on the naturalism of Danish novelist Jens Peter Jacobsen, and her innovative novels that were spiritual allegories—*Eyes* and *Seraph* ; Hurston, and Arna Bontemps also wrote historical novels, respectively "Herod the Great" and *Black Thunder*. Working in the long poem and the lyric poem Georgia Douglas Johnson, Jean Toomer, Melvin B. Tolson, and Gwendolyn Bennett produced an estimable body of esoteric poetry. While the Harlem writers were producing their coded esoteric texts, so were the white followers of Orage. Novelists in the Oragean Modernist mode of *esoteric realism* besides Carl Van Vechten included Dawn Powell, John Dos Passos, John O'Hara, Marjorie Kinnan Rawlings, Isa Glenn, Elinor Wylie, Walter Gilkyson, Nathaniel West, and James Agee. Djuna Barnes, though affiliated with The Rope, a group of American lesbians living in Paris that was in direct contact with Gurdjieff, wrote ciphered texts in the Oragean modernist mode, including her semi-canonical novel *Nightwood* (1936). The white Oragean Modernists are hard to talk about as a distinct group for a number of reasons. While the African American Oragean Modernists are well known in the context of the Harlem Renaissance, the white Oragean Modernists play out against the amorphous "Lost Generation." Some of the white Oragean Modernists have been associated with the "Lost generation" and some have not. But the "Lost Generation" has an indefinite membership and no real standing as a modernist literary movement in the sense of having been a definite group that fostered a manifesto and an aesthetic program. It is also doubtful that there were any distinctions within the Oragean Modernist organization—with everyone being equally inside of the esoteric school. As an example of the problems that arise, there is the case of the recent book on Marjorie Kinnan Rawlings and Zora Neale Hurston. Even for Anna Lillios, the author of the study, there is little perceived commonality between Rawlings and Hurston, and their coming together was improbable. Yet both were members of the Oragean Modernist group. Under a different set of assumptions about these writers, their writings will be found to have much in common, they will be found to know people in common, and their motivations will be found to be very different than the present scholarly understanding of them.

Finally, in the absence of a manifesto or a text that is identified as the Oragean Modernist ur-novel, the closet thing to a description of Orage's esoteric school is Van Vechten's esoteric comic novel, *Firecrackers*. *Firecrackers* is a *roman a clef* that described the founding of a branch of Gurdjieff's Institute in New York. The account calls the organization Pinchon's Prophylactic Plan, but the fictional prospectus that Pinchon (a character based on Orage's secretary, Muriel Draper) circulates actually mentions Gurdjieff and Ouspensky. What obtained among the Oragean Modernists was radically different from what Gurdjieff taught in France: Gurdjieff's demonstrations were performed in public, there was no writing commissioned by Gurdjieff and he took no interest in his students's writings, and never was his code—if there were one—divulged, though Orage and others searched long and hard for the key to his texts.

3. Oragean Modernism and "Experiment"

One of the problems of explicating Oragean Modernism is that it is based on a radical ethos; the esoteric tendency situates the creations of the esoteric worker such that the conventional reader is always at the disadvantage of absorbing material that is not accurate and that at times partakes of the absurd. No better example of this is Zora Neal Hurston's essay "The Characteristics of Negro Expression" published in the 1934 *Negro* anthology. So fundamental is this essay to the reading of the Hurston canon that one prominent critic even complains that the essay has been used "to provide a protocol for reading Hurston's novels" (Wall 4). Wall is at pains to argue that Hurston's essay itself is excessively florid:

> Retrospectively, critics have used these pieces, especially "Characteristics of Negro Expression," to provide a protocol for reading Hurston's novels. But we have paid inadequate attention to the formal qualities of the essays themselves. Although presented as field notes, "Characteristics" is suggestive formally as well as substantively. In the stories it recounts, "Characteristics" reflects the drama, to which Hurston gives priority among the elements of African American expression. The essay contains much evidence of the "will to adorn." Indeed, its profusion of metaphor and simile exist not only in the examples that are offered to support that observation, but throughout the essay itself. (Wall 4)

But despite Wall's interest in the essay she has not got the materials in hand to go beyond merely proposing that the essay is not doing a lot of definitive explication but is instead implicating the reader in the task of deciding what is to be learned about Negro expression: "Not only does it engage readers through its deployment of metaphor, it addresses them directly ("Who has not observed?") and indirectly ("Anyone watching Negro dancers"). In other words, the essay asks its readers to puzzle out its argument and to confirm the validity of its claims" (Wall 4). In the end Wall tries to move toward an appreciation of the essay without troubling herself to see that the essay reveals itself as nonsense on the surface and esoteric beneath the surface. And if Wall is taken in, it is done so against a more general disregard for anything that Hurston says. Hurston was discussing angularity in terms of the setting down of physical objects in random order, but Alice L. Birney strains this notion of angularity as a protocol for reading a Hurston play:

> *Cold Keener* (1930) is a "revue" with nine skits that are unrelated in their themes, characters, or even their settings, which include Georgia, Harlem, Florida, the Bahamas, and a jook joint. *Cold Keener* illustrates Hurston's concept of *"primitive angularity"* in dramatic structure—the parts are linked only by their differences. With this fresh approach, she hoped to challenge the African-American stereotypes derived from minstrel shows and thus contribute to the formation of a "real Negro theater." (Birney "Hurston and Her Plays; emphasis added)

Despite the quotation marks in the passage above, nowhere does Hurston actually say "primitive angularity," she says "angularity" and she does not modify it. And while Hurston appoints such a possibility for so abstract a notion as angular "dramatic structure," when she says "Everything that [the Negro] touches becomes angular. In all African sculpture and doctrine of any sort we find the same thing." (Hurston "Characteristics")— we have to realize that we do not know what she is talking about. Birney's explication of *Cold Keener* makes nonsense of the play and misuses Hurston's intentional nonsense as sense in order for Birney to compound her further nonsense. What in the first place is an angular doctrine? This is a good example of a "lawful inexactitude"—an instance where Hurston's says something absurd in order to make the reader aware of the hidden and esoteric level of her text. And is it indeed true that African architecture, dance and sculpture are more invested in angles than European forms? What for that matter are European and African forms? Hurston says this, but what proof is offered? None. She does not even give an example that can be used to argue this point that is acceptable: she says that there are angles in African dance but that Europeans avoid angles. Are there no angles in the postures of ballet? How is such a refusal to form angels attained, given the construction of the human body? And it is not true. Notre Dame is angular, and the Zulu *kraal* is symmetrical—circular and hemispherical.

My point here is that what Wall notices as Hurston's "will to adorn" is in actuality the means by which Hurston's essay has sidestepped the conventional anthropological form of expression that would have prevented her from writing her essay as an esoteric text. Hurston further troubles and complicates this disruption with an absurd discussion of secrecy: "It is said that Negroes keep nothing secret, that they have no reserve. This ought not to seem strange when one considers that we are an outdoor people accustomed to communal life. Add this to allpermeating [sic] drama and you have the explanation." The implication is that the essay broaches the subject of the secret because it is filled with secrets. Similarly, in *Turn, Magic Wheel* Dawn Powell says that a character is "nameless" in a passage in which a name is being presented in code. Because Hurston has disguised her esoteric text as an expressive hodgepodge of an essay, she has been able to adopt a language that allows her to densely encode the names of A.R. Orage, P.D. Ouspensky, G.I. Gurdjieff, and C. Daly King into her essay. She has also peppered the essay with Gurdjieffian terminology—all without directly alerting her readers to her complex subversion. The only thing amiss in this is that due to their habits of reading and analysis Hurston's critics are unable to penetrate to the coded level of her text. I will not go into detail with examples, but I will present a sampling of the esoteric content of Hurston's anthropological essay:

1. The Law of Three and the Law of Seven are fundamental to the Gurdjieff Work. Gurdjieffian writers habitually point to these laws by bringing the two numbers together, as in this sentence

from Hurston's essay: "There were seven calendars and three wall pockets."

2. The spiritual system that Gurdjieff taught was called the Fourth Way, because the "sly man" uses means that are more efficient than the monk, the ascetic, and saint—thus the Gurdjieff Work is a fourth "type" of spiritual practice. Hurston points to this through the double repetition of "forth" and "type" in this passage: "The sort of woman her men idealise is the *type* that is put *forth* in the theatre. The art-creating Negro prefers a not too thin woman, who can shake like jelly all over as she dances and sings, and that is the *type* he put *forth* on the stage." (emphasis added). "Type" is itself a particularly Gurdjieffian term, and Gurdjieff developed a study of the twenty-one types of human individualities that he called "the science of idiotism."

3. G.I. Gurdjieff's writings were read aloud in the group meetings. These writings were collected under the title, *All and Everything*. A close examination of Hurston's essay shows that it is rife with the word "all"—unnecessarily so. The word "everything" is emphasized throughout: "Everything is acted out."; "Everything illustrated."; "Everything that he touches becomes angular." The two words are brought together in this passage: "Everything that he touches becomes angular. In all African sculpture and doctrine of any sort we find the same thing."

4. The ability to decode Hurston's phonetic *cabala* is an acquired taste. It is read through the use of phonetics and reads in both directions. It also uses a rough form of the anagram and is so flexible that it is, in practical terms, indecipherable. Were this not true, Oragean Modernism would have been previously discovered. The difficulty of the phonetic *cabala* is such that I will merely present some examples and move on.

Here is the name "A.R Orage" given in one brief passage: "The stark, trimmed phrases of the Occident seem too bare for the voluptuous child of the sun, hence the adornment. It arises out of the same impulse as the wearing of jewelry and the making of sculpture--the urge to adorn."

In the following passage, Hurston takes a while to present the unassembled components of "Gurdjieff":

On the walls of the homes of the average Negro one always finds a glut of *gaudy* calendars, wall pockets and advertising lithographs. The sophisticated white man or Negro would tolerate none of these, even if they bore a likeness to the Mona Lisa. No commercial art for decoration. Nor the calendar nor the advertisement spoils the picture for this lowly man. He sees the beauty in spite of the declaration of the Portland Cement Works or the butcher's announcement. I saw in Mobile a room in which there was an over-stuffed mohair living-room suite, an imitation mahogany bed and *chiff* erobe, a console victrola. (Emphasis added)

The quotation below is a continuation of the paragraph from the above quotation. The names are given over and over, so the word "gaudy" appears below in the passage—and thus "chifferobe" is bracketed by "gaudy." The same unconstituted treatment is given Ouspensky" in the following passage, with only an approximation of the name suggested, something like ess-pen-esque-y, but the mention of the out of place fountain pen is a clear indication of a "lawful exactitude" that points to the existence of coded material:

Over the door was a huge lithograph showing the Trea*ty* of Versailles being signed with a Waterman fountain *pen*.

It was grotesque, yes. But it indicated the desire for beau*ty*. And decorating a decoration, as in the case of the doi*ly* on the gaudy wall pocket, did not seem out of place to the host*ess*.

What one carries away from this examination is the simple proposition that Zora Neal Hurston felt that it was worth it to make a charade of a scientific anthropological presentation because she felt that the stakes were so high that this sort of behavior was not extreme.

The Hurston examples above are from an isolated essay and so they do not speak to the Oragean Modernists's fundamental and general concern with subterfuge, conspiracy, and double-dealing. It is my hope that the assertions that I am making in this study can be borne out by examples found in the published writing of all of the Oragean Modernists, since their letters, diaries, and public statements cannot be trusted. I will therefore cite a short story, "A Prisoner of Memory," published in *Harper's Magazine* by Walter Gilkyson in 1930. The story is the account of a murder trial. An upper-class lawyer has been recruited by a judge to defend a young Italian immigrant man. Because the lawyer has sentimental associations with Italy and speaks Italian, the lawyer misses many clues that should have warned him that the whole affair is not on the level. Once he has freed the young man, the lawyer is brought to a celebration at a restaurant. Immediately things began to deteriorate, the greatest shock coming when the lawyer is awarded the murder weapon by the proprietor of the Calabrese Restaurant. The proprietor, who is described as being a demon, is Gilkyson's rendering of Gurdjieff. The lawyer soon realizes that all of the witnesses used to defend the accused murderer are employees of the restaurant and that the proprietor, who is described in such a way that he is unmistakably Gurdjieff, has organized and scripted the whole affair: he is the leader of a criminal underground. The exaggeratedly negative portrayal of Gurdjieff goes along with the tendency of Oragean Modernist politics to villainize Gurdjieff while adoring Orage. Of course, none of Gurdjieff's ideas are rejected, and the Oragean Modernists wholeheartedly embraced and even further extended the role of conspiracy in their group. But we see that the Oragean Modernists were so imbued with conspiracy and subterfuge that the centrality of secrecy and deception is readily apparent from reading their texts. Finally, it must be pointed out that the name of the restaurant, the Calabrese Restaurant, is a clue that the story uses the phonetic *cabala* so that it can carry a coded level.

4. Carl Van Vechten and his Comic Novels

Robert M. Crunden offers a rare treatment of Carl Van Vechten's fiction in *Body and Soul: the Making of American*

Modernism: Art, Music and Letters in the Jazz Age 1919-1926 (2000). An American Studies scholar, Crunden is grounded in a revisionist historiography, and he has drunk deeply of the queer theory and postmodernism Kool-Aid. His motive for examining Van Vechten seems to be the need to ridicule Van Vechten, and in that respect he serves very well as an introduction to the critical reception and analysis of Van Vechten's fiction. In the breezy and dismissive way that Crunden handles Van Vechten, Crunden states that "[Van Vechten] also put his friends in the book under pseudonyms, heaven knows why since they loved the attention" (184). This is the sort of thing that critics say, and what it means to me is that he has no idea of what Van Vechten is doing, but that it really does not matter. Crunden's handling of Van Vechten's fiction is slapdash: he first posits that "In terms of the written word, Van Vechten was actually at his best in a tetralogy of sorts that he published between 1922 and 1925" (183). Crunden somehow does not notice that Van Vechten was a prolific novelist —so I will point to that in passing. Crunden again establishes his incapacity in connection with the text that I will eventually discuss in some detail: "But *Firecrackers* is the best, somehow managing to be both the last work of American decadence and the first of postmodernism. The title page called it 'realistic novel,' which of course it couldn't possibly be" (186-7). This—while slinging categories about like a fan dancer—is as snide and evasive as to be entirely useless. And Crunden is one of the most sensitive critics of Van Vechten's novels. (It is worth recalling that Nella Larsen considered *Nigger Heaven* to be a realistic novel, though Van Vechten did not add that descriptor to the title of the novel. Being privy to the esoteric content of *Nigger Heaven*, Larsen knew that it was indeed realistic—in the sense of being "objective"—for in Oragean Modernist aesthetics, realistic and "objective" are equivalent terms. The encoding of esotericism into *Nigger Heaven* is quite intricate. The name Byron Kasson may be read as "Buridan's ass"—an allusion to Jean Buridan's satire of the determinism affirmed by Aristotle's treatise, "On the Heavens" [*De Caelo*]. The title of Van Vechten's novel is thus not as simple as it looks, for it suggests that there are several levels of wordplay intended—with Gurdjieff's initials G.I.G. suggested by "nigger" and the word "heaven" ringing changes through philosophy as well as through African-American culture.)

In *To Make a New Race* my study of the Harlem Renaissance and A.R. Orage's Gurdjieff groups, I established a link between Van Vechten and the New York Gurdjieff group by showing that Van Vechten's name was on the New York membership list. I also showed that Van Vechten was in close contact with Muriel Draper, who was one of his best friends and who was also Orage's secretary. Draper in effect ran the practical side of the Gurdjieff groups in New York and New Jersey. The chart below shows the network of the Oragean Modernist literary movement:

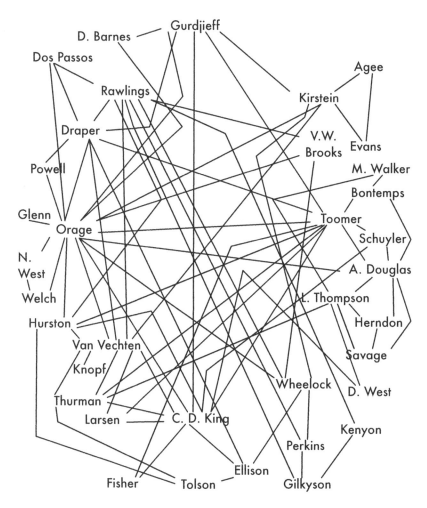

Tom Hodd states that

> Literary Modernism, and New Criticism specifically, has long been a source of frustration for scholars. Early critics who embraced the New Critical theory of textual autonomy without question (though perhaps unconsciously) have perpetuated a closed-minded approach towards a period of English literature that claims to have no outside influences—that the text is the only point of consideration. As a result, scholars who challenged this belief find themselves on the periphery of Modernist scholarship, struggling to demonstrate the validity of their contributions. A prime example of this "critical marginalization" is the field of occult scholarship.
>
> The stigma of the occult's associations with demon worship in Western culture and the prevailing theory of textual autonomy have weighed heavily on accepted pursuits of critical literary scholarship in Literary Modernism. Excepting W.B. Yeats, scholars have grossly ignored any relation the Modernists held to pagan religions, and in some instances, have blatantly denied the existence of a "secret tradition" in Modernist literature. Thus, occult commentary by early critics like F.L. Lucas, David Evans, William Tyndall or John Senior were, for the most part, simply dismissed as insubstantial pageants. But a group of recent critics is again challenging this conservatism: James Longenbach, Leon Surette, Timothy Materer, Leonora Woodman, Demetres Tryphonopoulos, and a host of other critics contend that the influence of the occult on late 19th century and early 20th century writers does indeed exist. Their studies attest to the fact that occult research should not remain on the periphery of "true" critical scholarship, but instead be moved into the mainstream of Modernist thought. (Hodd "Literary Modernism")

Hodd overstates the degree to which occult research has entered the mainstream of literary studies, for in recent years many of the figures that he names have abandoned this area of investigation. In contrast to the treatment of the influence of the occult on modern literature, there is a general understanding of the role of the occult in modern art. Hamilton Reed Armstrong gives this account of the occult side of modern art:

> According to the authors of *The Spiritual in Art, Abstract Painting 1890-1985,* a voluminous catalogue prepared for a show of Modern Art at the Los Angeles County Museum, the common denominator of the Modern Art hanging in prestigious galleries and museums today is the preoccupation of its producers with occult spirituality. The catalogue's list of artists who have dabbled in the occult is a "who's who" of Modern Art: Jean Arp, Marcel Duchamp, Augusto Giacometti, Adolf Gotlieb, Jasper Johns, Wassily Kandinsky, Ellsworth Kelly, Paul Klee, Piet Mondrian, Eduard Munch, Barnett Newman, Georgia O'eeffe, Jackson Pollack, Ad Reinhart, Mark Rothko, and Albert Pinkham Ryder, among a host of others. The catalogue also contains an appendix of the "occult" sources of these artists: Alchemy, Kabbalah, Hermeticism, Neoplatonism, Paracelcus, Jacob Boehm, Rosicrucianism, Spiritualism, Swedenborg, Shamanism, and Theosophy, among others. The common denominator of all of these systems according to Maurice Tuchman, organizer of this exhibition and its catalogue, is that they all share the following world view:
>
> > The universe is a single, living substance; mind and matter also are one; all things evolve in dialectical opposition; thus the universe comprises paired opposites (male-female, light-dark, vertical-horizontal, positive-negative), [sic] everything corresponds in a

universal analogy, with things above as they
are below; imagination is real; and self
realization can come by illumination, accident,
or an induced state.

(Armstrong "Modern Art and the Occult")

The greatest occultist of the nineteenth century was H.P.
Blavatsky, and the greatest occultist of the twentieth century was
G.I. Gurdjieff. There is a great deal of continuity and overlap
between the influences of these figures. Gurdjieff echoed
Blavatsky's aim to bring the science of the West and the religion of
the East together. For a specific instance of overlap, I will point to
a poem by Jean Toomer who is well known to have been a devotee
of Gurdjieff, yet "Blue Meridian," one of his most widely
anthologized and most highly regarded poems, is essentially a
paraphrase of the occult racial doctrines outlined in Blavatsky's
book, *The Secret Doctrine* (1888). The importance of Blavatsky to
Toomer's poem has escaped Toomer's critics, as knowledge of
occultism is a rare thing among literary scholars. One exception is

Tom Gibbons, Senior Lecturer in English at the
University of Western Australia, [who] wrote in his
Rooms in the Darwin Hotel (1974) — a study of ideas
current in English literature from 1880 to 1920 — that
Blavatsky and other theosophical writers attracted
intelligent readers because they "presented the human
situation as something complex, meaningful, and
exciting . . . and stress the importance of spiritual values
and free will." He was attracted by the theosophic claim
to reconcile religious belief with discoveries made by
scientists and also to open the door for *public* study of
non-Christian religions. (Oderberg "H. P. Blavatsky's
Cultural Impact)

Just as Blavatsky attracted many serious minds in her time,
Gurdjieff attracted a host of talented creators and thinkers, none

more highly regarded than A.R. Orage. The following is a standard exposition of Orage's life:

Alfred Richard Orage (born 22 January 1873, Dacre, Yorkshire, England—- died 6 November 1934, London) was a British intellectual, now best known for editing the magazine *The New Age.* While working as a schoolteacher in Leeds, he pursued various interests, including Plato, the Independent Labour Party, and theosophy. In 1900, Orage met Holbrook Jackson and three years later they co-founded the Leeds Arts Club, which became a centre of modernist culture in pre-World War I Britain. In 1905, Orage resigned his teaching position and moved to London. There, in 1907, he bought and edited the English weekly *The New Age*, at first with Holbrook Jackson, and became an influential figure in socialist politics and modernist culture, especially at the height of the magazine's fame before the First World War.

Between 1908 and 1914 *The New Age* was undoubtedly the premier little magazine in the UK. It was instrumental in pioneering the British avant-garde, from vorticism to imagism. Some of its contributors at this time included Wyndham Lewis , Herbert Read and many others. Apart from his undoubted genius as an editor, it might be said that Orage's real talent was as a conversationalist and a 'bringer together' of people. The modernists of London were scattered between 1905 and 1910. Between 1910 and 1914, largely thanks to Orage, a sense of a genuine 'movement' was created. In other words, Orage successfully ran a forum which at least assumed (and perhaps created) a commonality between the seemingly unfathomable philosophies and artistic practices then being created.

In 1924, A. R. Orage sold *The New Age* and went to France to work with the spiritual teacher P. D. Ouspensky had recommended to him. The teacher was George Ivanovitch Gurdjieff. After spending some time of preliminary training in the Gurdjieff System, Orage was sent to America by Gurdjieff himself to raise funds and lecture on the new system of self-development which emphasized the harmonious work of intellectual, emotional and moving functions. Orage also worked with Gurdjieff in translating the first version of Gurdjieff's *All and Everything* as well as *Meetings with Remarkable Men* from Russian to English; however, neither book was ever published in their lifetime. (Wikipedia)

In New York Orage used his considerable notoriety to great advantage to increase the membership in the Gurdjieff groups by organizing writing workshops. These workshops used Gurdjieff's doctrines as templates for writing assignments, and because Orage was a talented teacher and his pupils were many of the finest writers of the time, his workshop students produced many successful published works.

Here what is publicly known about the nature of the Oragean teachings comes to an end. Although Louise Welch has written an account of Orage's time in New York, it is obvious that the whole story has not been told. One indication of this is the fact that at one point Gurdjieff came to New York, fired Orage, and broke up his groups—saying that Orage depended too much on the technique of self-observation. Self-observation was one of the fundamental techniques used by Gurdjieff to awaken his followers, and Orage's classes introduced the technique of "self-observation without identification" almost from the first meetings of each course. Gurdjieff felt that Orage's concentration on this technique had made all of his New York students into "psychopaths." We cannot really know what any of this means, and an even further difficulty comes into play when Gurdjieff further accuses Orage of never taking his students beyond the exoteric level of the Fourth Way teachings: since anything beyond that level is esoteric and has not been divulged to the public, there is no way to evaluate this statement. My examination of the novels of the Harlem Group shows that these texts are driven largely by the concept of self-observation without identification. At the same time, it can be inferred that along with self-observation Orage must have emphasized the idea that the Earth was in crisis: the time had arrived for mankind to progress to another level or to be extinguished. Although this idea is fleetingly broached by Gurdjieff, it seems to be a hallmark of everything that went on in the New York groups. Ouspensky gives the example of the ant, which supposedly was larger and intelligent, but which was demoted for lack of the ability to supply the right nutrients to a higher level; the doctrine of Reciprocal Maintenance is that everything that exists in this world depends on other things for its maintenance and must in its turn maintain the existence of something else (Ouspensky, *In Search of the Miraculous* 182-92). An American Gurdjieff group in the Jane Heap lineage describes the relationship of the human race to the potential for development in these terms:

> Nature has brought us to the point where we are. We have a certain time when there is a possibility for development and if there is no change, no development, then such as we are, we are destroyed forever. This is a terrifying situation to be in, but we do not see it. Nature does everything to excess. For the great bulk of humanity there is not and never will be any chance to be other than they are—to be born, to live out their trifling lives, and to die, destroyed forever. Gurdjieff calls this "manure for the moon." *At the same time, a certain number of the human race must make the necessary efforts to develop. By so doing, the contribution made by our planet to the cosmic harmony is brought closer to what it should be.* (Two Rivers Farm "The Work; emphasis added)

It is my thesis that in concert with the early development of Orage's writing groups (some time around 1924) a new type of literature was developed. *The problem that this new form of literature presents is that in effect it does not exist.* Where we might expect to find a description of it, we find instead a description of an entirely different sort of activity. Even though some of the people who appear in the descriptions produced Oragean Modernist texts, there is no indication that under Orage's guidance there was a school of writers working from the same esoteric template. One of the most detailed accounts of how Orage addressed creative writing was provided by Gorham Munson:

> Occasionally he would converse on literature, and once after he had talked at some length about Meredith, an entranced light versifier exclaimed: "But why don't you write literary essays?" "I write writers," was the reply. That had been the truth about Orage during the fifteen years he had edited the Nero Age and grown famous as the discoverer and coach of new talents. It was even more true in America in 1927,1928 and 1929 when he did something not attempted in London and held private classes in journalism.
>
> Just as people who scorned going to lectures had flocked to the psychological groups, so professional writers, who scoffed at courses in writing, enrolled for Orage's lectures on the art of literature, submitted manuscripts, and salted away the knowledge of the defects he exposed with what he called "appropriate injustice" Some of the writers—like Lawrence S. Morris, chief reviewer for the New Republic; T. S. Matthews, future literary editor of Time; Isa Glenn, the novelist; Melville Cane, the poet; Oakley Johnson, the Communist journalist; John Riordan, Amos Pinchot, Muriel Draper — came from the psychological groups; others — Currie Matthews Cabot, Savington Crampton, Hansell Baugh, Genevieve Taggard, Dorothea Brande — came from outside and tasted the course for various lengths of time.

Orage would begin such a course by saying that he would like to discorage [sic] his hearers from the attempt to write, and he would therefore proceed to paint the difficulties of writing —which he did in such a way that no pursuit seemed more fascinating. His method was the reverse of Quiller-Couch's lectures on writing which began with a picture of the heights of literature raising to Shakespeare, putting the class on its knees, and then ascended to the Bible, prostrating the class. Orage began with journalism and not until the final lectures did he disclose the Himalayas. He humanized the craft of letters before divinizing the art of literature, concentrating on first evoking a doing attitude, a practical outlook, on the part of his prentice writers. ("Orage in America")

Munson does not say that Orage's students wrote esoteric novels. A large number of writers under Orage's guidance actually produced esoteric novels. In Munson's account, only Isa Glenn is specifically mentioned as a novelist; Glenn was never a successful novelist, and she is a poor example of the reception of Orage's creative writing students—several of whom won national acclaim for their esoteric novels. In another list Munson also mentions the historical novelist Mary Johnston as having attended Orage's lectures, but she is not designated as a writing student. It appears that the actual nature of the Oragean Modernist writing group was never publicly divulged. What can be said about the activities of the Oragean Modernists writers is based on extracting information from what they published—both in terms of what they may have said about themselves and what can be concluded from what is known about their movements and affiliations.

My assumption is that the primary creators in this new literary mode were the mystery writer C. Daly King and the comic novelist Carl Van Vechten. Academic scholars have not noticed the occult nature of their literary works. Both writers employed figures from their own Gurdjieffian milieu, and both writers have ciphered their occult doctrines using the traditional code of the alchemists. These texts are only lightly coded, so once it is clear that there is a code involved, the code is easily penetrated. And one feature of all of these texts is that the authors were using many techniques (vocabulary—secret, cipher, code, "legominism;" repetition; self-referentiality—someone in the text using a code; "lawful inexactitudes;" and suspiciously misspelled words) to betray the existence of the code. However, it seems that without prior knowledge of the code, the common reader—even when a literary scholar—is unable to detect the code.

This so-called phonetic *cabala* is well known in occult circles, and it is not the invention of Orage or of his circle. The *cabala* was introduced into the attention of the modern world through the modern alchemist Fulcanelli's books *Mystery of the Cathedrals* (*Le Mystere des Cathedrales*) and *Dwellings of the Philosophers* (*Les Demeures Philosophales*), first published in French in Paris in 1926 and 1929 respectively. *Cabala* is Fulcanelli's term for a special use of language, drawing on phonetic similarities and other symbolic techniques for expanding the expressive reach of words. The *cabala* is equivalent to the Green Language or Language of the Birds of the medieval alchemists. Fulcanelli's books were published by his pupils Eugene Canseliet and Jean-Julien Champagne. Fulcanelli's books are themselves prime examples of multilayered language and *cabala*. Fulcanelli is a mysterious person about whom nothing is know, and for all we know there was direct contact between Carl Van Vechten and Fulcanelli or some member of his circle. When Van Vechten was a music critic prior to his career as a novelist, for many years he traveled to Paris for concerts. In any case, the Oragean Modernists came into contact with the phonetic *cabala*, and they made consistent use of it in their published texts.

Lest the association of the phonetic *cabala* to the occult estrange the Oragean Modernists, it must be pointed out that this way of handling language is described by linguists as "metathesis." Metathesis is the re-arranging of sounds or syllables in a word, or of words in a sentence. Most commonly it refers to the switching of two or more contiguous sounds, known as adjacent metathesis or local metathesis. Metathesis may also involve switching non-contiguous sounds, known as nonadjacent metathesis, long-distance metathesis, or hyperthesis. While metathesis is not as common as other processes affecting sounds in language, such as assimilation or deletion, it does, nonetheless, occur as a regular phonological process in synchronic systems in a wide range of languages (Hume "Metathesis"). Thus, metathesis is a "natural" linguistic process that takes place in the mutation of spoken language. All the alchemists have done is to give special emphasis to this process so that it becomes a practical cryptographic technique.

At the age of forty music critic Carl Van Vechten began writing novels: *Peter Whiffle* (1922), *The Blind Bow-Boy* (1923),*The Tattooed Countess* (1924),*Firecrackers. A Realistic Novel* (1925), *Excavations* (1926), *Nigger Heaven* (1926), *Spider Boy* (1928), and *Parties* (1930). The novels were praised by critics and were bestsellers. Crunden is correct about one thing—the blurring of the "real" and the "imaginary" (184) that is characteristic of Van Vechten's handling of New York society. But critics like Crunden run all of Van Vechten's novels together, even though there is a distinction to be made between two groups of them—the non-realistic and the realistic. In contrast to Crunden's presentation of the arc of Van Vechten's fictional production, there must have been two series of novels, one prior to his interest in Gurdjieff and one subsequent. Since Gurdjieff was only interested in works of "objective" art, Van Vechten would have distinguished his "subjective" novels from his "objective" novels. Since Van Vechten only encountered the Fourth Way in 1924, his early novels would by necessity have to be "subjective." This means that the series of novels written after he became a Gurdjieffian [*Firecrackers. A Realistic Novel* (1925), *Excavations* (1926), *Nigger Heaven* (1926), *Spider Boy* (1928), and *Parties* (1930)] were "objective." It is likely that Van Vechten signaled this aesthetic break between the "subjective' and the "objective" by calling *Firecrackers a "realistic" novel* , since he could not title it an "objective" novel.

Van Vechten's last five novels became the "esoteric realist" template for the novels of the Harlem group as well as for the other Oragean Modernists. While more will be said about the "esoteric realist" template, it must be pointed out here that the rapid production of novels by the Oragean Modernists was a central feature of their program. This program is described indirectly by Dawn Powell in *The Locusts Have No King*. The protagonist—the novelist Frederick Olliver—and his publisher are attending a party given by a rival publisher: " They examined in silence a special corridor lined with Beckley best sellers, each shelf equipped with a special light for close study of these nine day wonders. Determined to discover the secret of success Mr. Stafford spent several minutes searching for and adjusting his reading glasses and one minute in a swift glance up and down the collection, observing tersely that every fifth one was a historical novel " (20). The paragraph contains coded references to the whole Oragean Modernist "objective" drama, but I will let that go. What is stated on the surface is of greater interest. Dawn Powell has confronted the reader with "best sellers," "close study," and "nine day wonders." What I think this means is that Van Vechten's publisher, Alfred Knopf assisted Van Vechten in publishing best selling novels with an esoteric subtext that were written in brief spans of time. This is a good summation of what I am discussing in my study of Oragean Modernist fiction—a great number of best selling novels produced in rapid order by esotericists—thus the need for close study.

I was surprised to come across the mention of historical novels in Powell's novel, but I have now identified a group of Oragean Modernist writers who produced historical novels. While in the past I had written on Hurston's *Moses Man of the Mountain*, I had not thought of it as a historical novel. But once the idea that there were other such works became credible, I continued to pursue texts in that genre. The next one that I found was Arna Bontemps's *Black Thunder.* Bontemps met Margaret Walker on a WPA project in Chicago in the 1930s. Famously, Walker typed manuscripts for another WPA member, Richard Wright, but Walker also came under Bontemps's Oragean Modernist influence and turned her in-progress manuscript on slavery into the esoteric historical novel, *Jubilee* (1966). Walker's *Jubilee* had a very long gestation, taking more than twenty years to write and only coming into print during the cultural furor of the 1960s. I have since added Elinor Wylie to the roll of Oragean Modernists, and she was the author of a number of historical novels. Most recently I have come across the novels of Walter Gilkyson, whose *The Lost Adventurer* (1927) was set in the 1869 Spanish Revolution. It also remains to be seen if Mary Johnston's late novels are esoteric. Lincoln Kirstein's novel *Flesh Is Heir* (1931) is also considered a historical novel. So, the whole topic of esoteric historical novels remains to be explored.

Here I must insert a caveat, since some of the terminology that I am using is misleading. As I have demonstrated at great length in *To Make a New Race*, all of the literary productions of the Oragean Modernists were called by them "objective" but in reality (reality being in this case prescribed by the conditions of "objective" art as set forth by Gurdjiedff [8] and Ouspensky in their writings) all of their writings were "subjective." "Objective" art cannot be achieved by human beings who lack cosmic consciousness, thus the art of the Oragean Modernists, who Gurdjieff denounced as being *uninitiated psychopaths*[9], could never produce works of art that were truly "objective." This two-fold division of Van Vecten's novels into the "objective" and the "subjective" is confirmed by the depiction of the commencement of the Gurdjieff Work in *Firecrackers. A Realistic Novel* (1925)— which follows because Gurdjieff first appeared with his performing troupe in New York in 1924 to the acclaim of the entire New York intelligentsia. Despite its neglect by scholars, Van vechten's novel has some standing in its presentation of the 1920s, for Bruce Kellner is able to state that "Humorous, poignant, and ironic, *Firecrackers* boldly stands as one of the most definitive portraits on the excesses and recklessness of the Jazz Age" (Kellner 169). Bruce Kellner describes the novel as follows:

> *Firecrackers* is the least known of *Carl Van Vechten*'s novels, probably because it has never been reprinted and all of the others have, some several times. Of the four (out of seven) novels that deal directly with what he called *'the splendid drunken twenties'* in New York, *Firecrackers* was published at the heart of the period and comes closest to depicting the *Jazz Age* in all its variety.

After eighty years, the novel will strike many readers as quaint or mannered or camp (or all three), but *Van Vechten* subtitled it *'a realistic novel,'* and the hi-jinks from the period on which it reports are apparently accurate, although informed by a masked austerity. As early as 1925, *Van Vechten* saw the end in sight even if few others were looking ahead that far. Coming out in the same year as books as disparate as *Fitzgerald's The Great Gatsby* and *Loos's Gentlemen Prefer Blondes*, dealing with similar if markedly different milieus, *Firecrackers* bolsters our understanding of that strange decade. It extends the lives of some characters in *Van Vechten's* earlier novels, and it anticipates the frantic desperation depicted in his last one, *Parties* (1930), when the stock market crash brought the twenties to a thudding halt. (169)

What has certainly thrown off Van Vechten's critics is the subtitle *"a realistic novel,"*—which they have had to somehow correlate with the surface text: Kellner points out that the hi-jinks are accurately portrayed, and Crunden dismisses the idea of the novel's realism—"which of course it couldn't possibly be" (187). centers around a wide cast of characters whose lives are irrevocably changed by the mysterious Gunnar O'Grady in 1920s New York. Paul Moody, the protagonist, is a man who finds his life utterly tedious and uneventful in New York City. Moody tries to uncover the mystery of his young friend, Gunnar O'Grady, while also desperately seeking his own purpose in the world. Little does Moody know that his life and the lives of those around him are about to be changed forever (Kellner 169).

In *To Make a New Race* I show that the realism that Van Vechten's subtitle refers to is the "objective art" of Orage's Gurdjieff circle: the New York Gurdjieffians had redefined the qualities and purposes of the esoteric aesthetic and were obsessively producing popular esoteric novels with which to disseminate their program. Gurdjieff stated that "The difference between objective art and subjective art is that in objective art the artist really does 'create,' that is he makes what he intended, he puts into his work whatever ideas and feelings he wants to put into it. And the action of this work upon men is absolutely definite; they will, of course each according to his own level, receive the same ideas and the same feelings that the artist wanted to transmit to them. There can be nothing accidental either in the creation or in the impressions of objective art" (Ouspensky ISM 295-97). The most obvious "objective" attribute is the use of the phonetic *cabala*. The code of the alchemists is called for at the opening of the novel, for when Paul Moody goes into his basement, he finds that the furnace repairman is reading the Sufi mystical text *The Alchemy of Happiness*. Gurdjieff is nearly always associated with Sufism and alchemy by the New York circle. Some sources maintain that it was the Sufis who originated the phonetic *cabala* in order to encode information for initiates.

If we apply the phonetic *cabala* to what we have so far, the title *Firecrackers*—which is an unsuitable title— can be read as a rough anagram for *sacrifice*. The rough anagram is exactly what is meant by saying that the phonetic *cabala* uses "phonetic similarities and other symbolic techniques." Sacrifice is indeed a concept presented by Gurdjieff in his own terms:

> "Sacrifice is necessary," said G. "If nothing is sacrificed nothing is obtained. And it is necessary to sacrifice something precious at the moment, to sacrifice for a long time and to sacrifice a great deal. But still, not forever. This must be understood because often it is not understood. Sacrifice is necessary only while the process of crystallization is going on. When crystallization is achieved, renunciations, privations, and sacrifices are no longer necessary. Then a man may have everything he wants. There are no longer any laws for him, he is a law unto himself." (Ouspensky 274)

The name Paul Moody is another type of wordplay that is easily read as "all doom." This is not grammatical, but it is clear in its meaning. As I have shown above, the central theme of Orage's teaching was that it was the purpose of the esoteric community to save the Earth by generating the proper form of vibrations that were required from the Earth: failure to supply this higher food would condemn the Earth to destruction. Thus Paul Moody's name is shorthand for the doctrine of Reciprocal Maintenance that states that everything that exists in this world depends on other things for its maintenance and must in its turn maintain the existence of something else. Gunnar O'Grady's name is an intriguing *cabala* of the combined names A.R. Orage, G.I. Gurdjieff, and perhaps even Jean Toomer. As the O'Grady figure is a blend of these three men, it is difficult to assign him one identity. He is however, a handsome acrobat, and this rather fits the figure that Jean Toomer cut at that time of his life: the former physical education teacher was teaching the Gurdjieff dances in Greenwich Village to the New York circle in addition to organizing a Gurdjieff workshop in Harlem. The names held over from former novels also turn out to be wordplay, but not of an esoteric caliber: for instance Campaspe Lorilard may be read as "railroad compass," indicating the surveying instrument used to lay out railroad tracks. Thus Van Vechten's pseudonyms seem to develop from camp word games into esoteric seriousness. The most important new character is the girl prodigy, Consuelo, who is the agent of truth that each of these novels contains. Her name may be read as "soul," not directly a Gurdjieffian concept. Van Vechten is more than likely using Consuelo to point to Gurdjieff's concept of essence:

> "If essence is very little developed, a long preparatory period of work is required and this work will be quite fruitless if a man's essence is rotten inside or if it develops some irreparable defects. Conditions of this kind occur fairly often. An abnormal development of personality very often arrests the development of essence at such an early stage that the essence becomes a small deformed thing. From a small deformed thing nothing else can be got. "Moreover, it happens fairly often that essence dies in a man while his personality and his body are still alive. A considerable percentage of the people

we meet in the streets of a great town are people who are empty inside, that is, they are actually *already dead*." (164)

Because she is a prodigy, Consuelo is in danger of developing a warped life, a danger that is discussed by some of the characters—though naively. The danger that she runs is made clear in the teachings: she is being raised by people who are destroying her essence.

When *Firecrackers* opens, Paul Moody is falling asleep over a novel—a novel that reflexively mocks the protagonist: this motif also occupies the opening scene of Nella Larsen's *Quicksand.* And as in Larsen's novel, Larsen's protagonist is reading a novel about the Near East, a novel that touches on the same themes presented in the opening of Van Vechten's novel, once Gunnar O'Grady has been discovered in the cellar. Given the documented closeness between Van Vechten and Larsen, it is not a stretch to argue for a connection between these texts. (The same thing may eventually be said about other novels by the Harlem Group. But this research needs to be done.) Van Vechten's esoteric novels are centered on the theme of essence and personality. (A similar interest in the development of young people is shared by other Oragean Modernists—Marjorie Kinnan Rawlings, Bernice Lesbia Kenyon, and James Agee being salient examples.) In *Parties*—a novel that seems entirely frivolous and intended to be one interminable joke —there is a scene in which the most dissolute character in the novel arranges for the visit of a psychic to entertain her drunken friends. The psychic has the power to strip away the artificial personas, the sub-personalities of the partygoers and to reveal their essences. This episode has clearly had no effect on Van Vechten's critics. Similarly, the parallel episode in *Firecrackers* was passed over by Crunden, who sees it as having something to do with what he calls Van Vechten's "androgynous style":

Like most of Van Vechten's work, the book seemed weightless even if amusing, until suddenly, like a theatrical device, a curtain fell away. Here it came on page seventy-one, when Edith Dale sent Campaspe Lorillard a letter about a friend, who had just published a little tract, "The Importance of the Facade." Just as Eugene O'Neill was rediscovering the potential modernity of the use of Greek masks, so Van Vechten was theatrically toying with "the basic principle of facial integrity," or how "any meditative person like you or me learns from our own insides how to make our faces." The allusion to Whistler and the use of makeup were fairly obvious; the pamphlet instructed us in "the gentle art of making faces." (187)

The passage is a "legominism" addressed to the teachings about the esoteric idea that the fundamental human condition is artificial —a central idea carried along by the idea that people wear masks. The references to "meditative" and "integrity" point towards the esoteric idea of having "one I." At the heart of Van Vechten's subterfuge is the idea that normal human beings lack a central identity, that they do not "remember themselves." In the passage quoted below, Ouspensky is quoting Gurdjieff:

"Self-observation becomes observation of 'Ouspensky.' A man understands that he is not 'Ouspensky,' that 'Ouspensky' is nothing but the *mask* he wears, the part that he unconsciously plays and which unfortunately he cannot stop playing, a part which rules him and makes him do and say thousands of stupid things, thousands of things which he would never do or say himself.

"If he is sincere with himself he feels that he is in the power of 'Ouspensky' and at the same time he feels that he is not 'Ouspensky.'" (Ouspensky 148; emphasis added)

By contrast with Crunden's dismissal of *Firecrackers*, an esoteric close reading of the novel shows that there is within the text a great deal of serious detail. It was Muriel Draper who organized the New York Gurdjieff school for Orage; in the novel she is presented as Emmeline Pinchon. "Emmeline Pinchon" is *cabala* for "pinch me," as in "pinch me, I must be dreaming"—a formula that makes sense in the context of the Gurdjieffian so-called "war against sleep." Draper's importance to the New York Orageans is consistent with Van Vechten's fictional depiction of her as Pinchon in *Firecrackers*:

> The following afternoon, as soon as she was free from the lessons she was engaged to impart to Consuelo, Miss Pinchon paid a visit to the Public Library where she devoted herself to a more or less extensive examination of curious works by Ouspensky and Arthur E. Waite. Further, she drew up a list from the catalogers of volumes on Hindu philosophy and noted down the titles of pamphlets dealing with Gurdjieff, Jaques-Dalcroze, and Einstein. A few of these she later purchased for home study. Within a week, a week of intensive research, she had evolved, with plagiarism here and there, and a limited use of the imagination, a philosophy of acrobatics which would suit her purpose and which, she was convinced, not unjustifiably, would make her fortune. Deep breathing while standing on the head during the simultaneous consideration of the ultimate oneness of God with humankind, the essential co-ordination of the waving left arm with the soul, and the identity of the somersault with the freedom of the will were a few of the attractive determining principles in this new mental-physical science which she dubbed, following the fashion of previous innovators along these lines, Pinchon's Prophylactic Plan. (173-74)

Though comic in its effect, Van Vechten's treatment of the governess's scheme points directly to Orage and The Institute for the Harmonious Development of Man, as Gurdjieff called his organization. The descriptions of the exercises is a lighthearted parody of the system of movements that Gurdjieff taught; while the movements were being done the student had to be conscious of what the body was sensing. The flyer that Pinchon draws up to advertise her offering—

> Miss Emmeline Pinchon
> announces the opening of her school
> for the propagation of
> her own mental-physical method
>
> PINCHON'S PROPHYLACTIC PLAN
> at 107 East Fiftieth Street
> Lessons in class: Two lessons a week for ten weeks: $200
> Private lessons: Two lessons a week for ten weeks: $400
> Reference: Mr. George Everest Telephone: Sahara 6897

—is in imitation of Gurdjieff's advertisement:

> From this point of view our psychic life, both as regards our world perception and our expression of it, fail to present an unique and indivisible whole, that is to say a whole acting both as a common repository of all our perceptions and as the source of all our expressions. On the contrary, it is divided into three separate entities, which have nothing to do with one another, but are distinct both as regards their functions and their constituent substances. These three entirely separate sources of the intellectual, emotional and instinctive or moving life of man, each taken in the sense of the whole set of functions proper to them, are called by the system under notice the *thinking, the emotional, and the moving centres*. (IHDM brochure; emphasis added)

Pinchon has substituted "mental-physical" for Gurdjieff's "the thinking, the emotional, and the moving centres."

5. The Oragean Modernist Ur-text

In *To Make a New Race*, my discussion of the novels written by the followers of A.R. Orage who participated in the Harlem Renaissance, my findings were based on an incomplete understanding of the scope of the Oragean Modernist movement. While I thought at the time that I was applying a radical revision to the understanding of the Harlem Renaissance—the conventional reading being that while it was a disparate movement with generational, ideological, and aesthetic fractures, the Harlem Renaissance was fundamentally unified by being entirely grounded in nationalism—my attempt to register the Harlem Renaissance as signally an opposition between nationalism and occultism blinded me to any links that extended beyond the Harlem writers. This was possible because I did not realize the role that Carl Van Vechten had played in determining the type of novel that was written by the Harlem group. Additionally, I was not aware that the Harlem Oragean Modernists were but one of the many literary subgroups that A.R. Orage had organized. This oversight was largely due to the published account of A.R. Orage's groups in New York: at no point does the portrait emerge of Orage having set up the kind of formal literary apparatus that is evident once a record has been assembled from combining the published historical accounts with the contents of Oragean Modernist fiction.

One of the curiosities of the Harlem Renaissance is that Jean Toomer's *Cane* is considered highly important to the initiation of the movement, yet the writers of the Harlem Renaissance rejected the lyrical impressionist style in which Toomer wrote *Cane*. Toomer himself soon abandoned the lyrical impressionist style. Toomer's unpublished novels, "The Gallonwerps" and "Transatlantic," more resemble the comic novels of the Oragean Modernists than they do his former writings. In *To Make a New Race* I gave a list of the common features of the Harlem renaissance novels of "esoteric realism." What I propose to do now is to provide a similar list, so that by working backwards from the writings of the Oragean Modernists, it might be possible to arrive at the delineation of an Oragean Modernist "ur-text" that will provide some idea of what the Orageans Modernists must have circulated among their circle of writers in order to end up with the sort of novels and stories that they produced.

Hypothesis: The Plan of the Oragean Modernist Esoteric-Realist, Comic-Satiric Novel:

1. The numbers three, eight, nine (the enneagram), and twenty-four (3x8=24) were important in G.I. Gurdjieff's cosmology. The cosmos was said to consist of "three degrees of radiation" or "three octaves." Following this template, the text might be divided into octaves or a series of octaves. Djuna Barnes's *Nightwood* has eight (8) sections. Van Vechten's *Nigger Heaven* has 9 chapters in Book 1 and 8 chapters in Book 2. The Harlem group was very faithful to this device, but the other groups were less constrained by it. (One of the frustrations of writing about the occult is that it is impossible to know where to draw a limitation. Some commentators would suggest that some Oragean Modernist novelists were using geometric addition or other forms of number symbolism. Thus the 26 chapters in Powell's *Turn, Magic Wheel* could be interpreted as 26=2+6=8. And the 19 chapters of Gilkyson's *The Lost Adventurer* might simply indicate the enneagram, where 19 means 1-9. If this approach is taken, there is a lot of material to speculate about, but it is not a useful line of inquiry.)

2. Important personalities from the esoteric community will appear as characters in the texts. In the Oragean Modernist writings Gurdjieff often appears—but as a villain. At times a character who resembles Orage will be placed in opposition to the Gurdjieff villain.

3. The text will be a "legominism"—a text within a text—in which the fundamental concepts in the system are presented. Legominism was a word used by Gurdjieff and was based on the Greek word for reading; thus a legominism has to do with instructing the reader how to read the text. In Oragean Modernist texts the word "legominism" is often presented through the *cabala* in order to alert the reader that what follows the clue will be a legominism—

an embedded esoteric text. At time merely the word "leg" suffices to indicate the entire word "legominism," and in others the word is only approximated, such as "let's go." Some writers will create more elaborate word games with the word "legominism." As with all "legominisms," the special nature of the text is indicated through the use of "lawful inexactitudes," or as Margaret Naumburg called them in a letter to Jean Toomer, "conscious discrepancies" (JTC Box 7t Folder 18). For example in "The characteristics of Negro Expression" Hurston mentions the Declaration of Independence being signed with a Waterman fountain pen. The "legominism" is handled in different ways by the various writers. At times there will be an embedded esoteric text that is bracketed by the word "legominism" (given indirectly). At other times the entire text will be a "legominism," with esoteric material presented as the vocabulary of the text. Some of the words that are "esoteric" in intention include work, remember, machine, shock, observe, law, food, Moon, fourth (for Fourth Way), sly, disguise, sleep, light, method.

The esoteric themes included in the bracketed off "legominisms" include: superman, seven types of men, one "I," evolution, involution, sleep, mechanical living, mental freedom, man is a prisoner but does not know it, man is a three-story factory, individuality, mask, playing a role, false personality, Ray of Creation, three octaves of radiation, law of three, and the law of the octave.

4. The text will perform an "attack on reading." The text is its own gloss, explicating the means by which it may be read. Included in the attack are such features as characters who are demonstrably incompetent readers; references to unreadable writing, ciphers and wordplay (codes, double talk, puns, clues, syllepses); intertextuality; intratextuality; archaeology of textual figures (textiles, veils, alcoves, houses, rooms, clothes); inscriptions (allegories, chalkboards, calligraphy, signs, manuscripts, paintings); proper names; emblematics; hieroglyphics; represented textuality to orality; represented textuality to corporeality; shifts of consciousness; absurdity; textual artificiality (pseudo-resistant

texts); textual self-referentiality; textual indeterminacy, and textual obliteration (self-consuming texts and self-destroying texts)—as when the draft of a novel is dropped into a bathtub and the ink is dissolved off of the pages at the end of *Infants of the Spring*.

5. *Cabala*. The text is written in the code called the phonetic *cabala*. This phonetic *cabala* is not to be confused with the Jewish Kabbalah. The word *cabala* often appears in Oragean Modernist texts: Melvin Tolson actually uses the word without disguise in *Harlem Gallery*:

> The Curator and Doctor Nkomo
> sat staring into space,
> united like the siphons of a Dosinia--
> the oddest hipsters on the new horizon of Harlem,
> odder
> by odds)
> than that
> cabala of a funeral parlor
> in Cuernavaca,
> Mexico
> called...
> "Quo Vadis."
> (lns. 2851-62).

In "The Man from Halicarnassus" he makes sure to specify that by *gabbalah* he means *cabala*, for he says "The *gabbalah* syllabled in Etruscan caves" (76) —indicating the specifically phonetic character of the code. In another long poem his presentation is indistinct: *cabala* may be heard by means of disparate syllables spread throughout the first stanza of the *Libretto for the Republic of Liberia,* so that it is barely perceptible. For instance, the "ba" in *cabala* comes in line 36: "No lamb to tame a lion with a baa."

In "E. & O. E." Tolson strains the limits of readability with a system of *cabala* that uses two words to sound out another word. In line 300 the opposing "jaws" of the Straits of Gibraltar, "Calpe and Abila," combine to say *cabala*: using this key: "Jean" can be extracted from "juices oceanic" (ln. 324) and combined with "tumorous" (ln. 326) to read "Jean Toomer."

The word *cabala* appears in each of Tolson's long poems, so that anyone aware of the nature of this alchemical code could decipher his poems. Walter Gilkyson headquarters his Gurdjieffian villain in the Calabrese Restaurant in his short story "The Prisoner of Memory." Dawn Powell presents the word indistinctly in *The Locusts Have No King*: "...hail a cab, but, after all..." (159). The *cabala* is the ancient code used by the European medieval alchemists. The code is very simple, but because it operates phonetically, and no one reads in this exact manner, it is practically speaking completely invisible. Were this not true, the use of *cabala* by the Oragean Modernists would have already been detected. There is surprisingly little written on the methods by which this code has been used; even the modern alchemist Fulcanelli, who was responsible for the revival of the *cabala*, is less than helpful, saying that this phonetic, spoken cabala is the same as the punning slang common to all languages and used by all outsiders to mask their communications from the others. Don Foster has given the most exhaustive explication of the rules of the *cabala*:

1. Consider the basic meanings of words and phrases..... MEANINGS MAY BE MULTIPLE, Eg., "My yoke is easy, but my burden is LIGHT." "He who CASTS the first stone,..........."

2. PREFIXES. Eg., Cover / DIScover

3. ROOT ORIGIN OF WORDS. A basic knowledge of Latin, Greek and Hebrew roots is very helpful. Eg., Origin = Ora/Aura - Gin/Gen, literally means the GENeration of gold or of something precious.

4. WORDS SOUNDING THE SAME but of different spelling. The phonetics of words becomes more important than their spelling. Looking for a common

meaning among words sounding the same or very similar. Eg., Rain / Reins (2 meanings.. kidneys + Horses' reins) / Reign / Rey (Spanish) / Ray / Pray / grain / drain / crane (2 meanings) / rhine / brain / spray / stray / strain / prey / quarry (2 meanings) / terrain / urine / train, etc..... common meaning associated with RADIATION or that which radiates from a source.

Mire / Mirror / Maya (Sanscrit) / Mirth .... common association with delusion, reflection, lost in unreality. This guide often holds when crossing language and transcultural barriers, ie. similar sounds can often have similar root meanings in French, Sanscrit, Norwegian, English, Creole, whatever.

5. Words or SOUNDS Within Words..... Eg.1. -ar- .... pertaining to fire and that which radiates upwards.

Non-exhaustive word list... aries, aryan, arabian, arak, arid, area, arena, arson, arsenal, art, artist, artery, arthroma, arthritis, arthrosis, article, arms, armour, ardour, arbour, arch, archer, arrow, architect, ark, argent, arsenic, car, carrot, cart, carcer, carcinoma, czar, earth, ear, farina, fart, garfish, garrot, harbour, hear, heart, hearth, hart, hark, harm, harmony, incarcerate, incinarate, mars, marshal, market, mark, park, part, party, para, pare, pear, raj, rajah, ra, ram, rare, rarify, smart, spar, spark, star, start, stark, starch, tartar, tart, target, war, warm, swarm, etc.

Eg.2. -or-, -ore-, -our-, -aur-, -augh-, -oar-, -aw-, -ory.... meaning pertaining to something precious, of great value, gold, light, central.

Non-exhaustive list of words.... ore, oar, awe, aura, aurora, aural, aurum, auditory, auger, ardour, absorb, arbour, bore, boar, calor, colour, core, coeur, courage, corn, cork, corona, coronet, court, caught, course, c'or, coral, chore, chorus, door, d'or, dolor, adore, dorado, floor, fort, flora, fortune, furor, gore, glory, harbour, hoary, horse, implore, juror, janitor, jailor, l'or, lore, law, labour, laboratory, mentor, more, maw, naught, knaw, organ, orgasm, oratory, orb, orbit, port, poor, porch, roar, raw, rubor, sailor, scorch, slaughter, shore, store, story, spore, sore, tor, tora, toro, torso, torch, tumour, valour, wor, whore, ordeals,

6. Basic letter sounds which have distinct meanings as well as unconscious archetypal associations. An example is the 3 Hebrew Mother letters of Shin (S) (Fire), Aleph (A) (Air) and Mem (M) (Water). The M.. sound is universally used beginning many words associated with water, nourishment, the receptive, the feminine, mother, matter.... check this out for yourself. LOOK TO THE SHAPES OF THE LETTERS THEMSELVES ALSO.

Do you think the Big-M sign on some establishments might have some unconscious suggestion of nourishment universally?

The letter X is associated with fixation, to raise vibrations, fusion of opposites, radiation, materialization, to increase, crucifixion, union of above with below, crossed wires.

The letter C is associated with concentration, focussing, en-closing, concentering..... Hence core, coeur, c'or, court (4 meanings), caught, crab, cancer, carcer, carcinoma, corps, corporation, carriage, car, coral, corral, crown, coronet, corn, cork, chorus, etc.

7. Words nearly sounding the same AND associated words. Eg., Evaluation / Reevaluation / Revelation. Word / Ward / World. Crow / Crown / Crone. Disciple /

Discipline. Table / Tablet / Stable. Vase / Urn. Vein / Venous / Venus / Vain.

8. Polarity Within Words. Eg., Male / Female. Bath / Bathe.

9. Combinations of the above.

If these guidelines above are applied only in an analytical fashion, little illumination is forthcoming, and it does all become a word game or 'play upon words'. But when the right side of the brain uses this knowledge intuitively, increasing realisations and understanding occurs, and it needs to be understood that alchemy is also about the WORD, sound, language, creation, evolution, awareness, consciousness. It is the fountainhead of ALL knowledge and art.

(Don Foster "The Alchemy Academic Forum." 201-250)

Far from being a casual aspect of the text, the use of *cabala* is constant. The names of G.I. Gurdjieff, A.R. Orage, P.D. Ouspensky, C. Daly King, and Jean Toomer are the text itself. The surface text is a palimpsest through which the names can be read constantly.

6. Genre.

Oragean Modernism was active during a time when there were active avant-garde literary movements, and indeed the membership of the Oragean Modernist group overlapped that of the Others group, the "Lost Generation," and similar groups of experimental writers and artists. Thus while the novel was being reformed according to the esthetics of such experimental movements as futurism, impressionism, expressionism, surrealism, and cubism, despite those potential influences, the genre most characteristic of Oragean Modernist writing was the realist comic-satiric novel. Besides the numerous comic novels by the Harlem Renaissance writers and those of Carl Van Vechten, in the category of the comic-satiric novel by Oragean Modernists, there are the novels of C. Daly King, Dawn Powell, Isa Glenn, Elinor Wylie, Nathaniel West, Ralph Ellison, and Walter Gilkyson.

The writer responsible for the innovations in the comic novel that the Oragean Modernist pursued was Ronald Firbank who began to publish about 1915. Firbank influenced Carl Van Vechten, and Van Vechten passed this comic style onto the Oragean Modernists. Humphrey Carpenter gives this account of the construction of a new type of modern novel that he distinguishes from the work of P.G. Wodehouse:

Another figure to appear on the literary scene at the same period offered definite hints of a possible way forward in comic writing. Ronald Firbank's novels began to come into print in 1915, and soon gained a small but loyal audience, Waugh among it. Firbank, imitated in *Broom* and other university periodicals by Acton and Howard, was part of the ambience of Waugh's Oxford. Betjeman says that the books, on his shelf in his rooms in Magdalen included '*Crome Yellow* [by Aldous Huxley], *Prancing Nigger* [by. Firbank], Blunden, Keats'. In an essay written not long after the publication of *Decline and Fall*, Waugh unhesitatingly identifies Firbank as a major influence on several contemporary writers, and by implication on himself : 'In quite diverse ways Mr. Osbert Sitwell, *Mr Carl Van Vechten*, Mr Harold Acton, Mr William Gerhardi and Mr Ernest Hemingway are developing the technical discoveries upon which Ronald Firbank so negligently stumbled.'

What were these discoveries? First, that it was not necessary to tell a story according to what Waugh called 'the chain of cause and effect'. In Firbank's fiction, events take place seemingly haphazardly, and appear to have been selected at the author's whim. Only gradually does their function in the story become apparent, and it is from this gradual unveiling of the scheme that much of the humour is derived. Firbank also discovered that it is possible to convey considerable intricacies and nuances of human relationships through dialogue cut to the bone. As Cyril Connolly says, 'When something bored him, he left it out (a device which might have improved the quality of innumerable novelists).' (Carpenter 152; emphasis added)

7. Esoteric contents.

The material that made up the Oragean version of the Gurdjieff Work is unfamiliar to most people. The introductory course of lectures gave the participants a grounding in psychology, metaphysics, and practical training. In order to bring the reader into some familiarity with these ideas, I am reproducing below the list of exercises that was given to the participants in Orage's groups in Harlem in 1926. This list of exercises was taken from a notebook that was kept by Jean Toomer and was found among his papers. It is of particular importance to notice that the exercises fall under the general heading of "self-observation and non-identification." All of the exercises are part of the endeavor of allowing the student to achieve mastery of the technique of "self-observation and non-identification." In the discussion of the writings of the Oragean Modernists that follow, I will be pointing out the ways in which the esoteric materials of the Oragean version have been introduced into their texts, and it is the vocabulary and exercises below that are often presented in their writings. Thus when a passage in John O'Hara's *Appointment in Samarra* says "Whenever he was on a party and did not drink too much he needed a secret game to play or a mental task to perform the while he was observing the amenities" (85), we are to understand that this is a veiled reference to "self-observation and non-identification." The game that Julian English is playing is to compare the woman he has married to another woman: thus the secret observation that he is making is entirely a matter of identification, not of non-identification. In fact it seems that

O'Hara's entire novel is little more than a rendering of the technique of "self-observation and non-identification" performed in the wrong way—that is, with identification. The result of this practice is that it has made Julian English into a psychopath, which is exactly what Gurdjieff said would happen even if the exercise were done in the correct manner but with a wrong emphasis.

Exercises

First and Last: self-observation and non-identification
1. The effort to realize: I have a body.
2. The effort to realize that I descended into and became attached to this organism (this animal) for the purpose of developing it.
3. The attempt to realize the organism's mechanicality.
    (a) Its habitual reaction to recurrent situations,
    (b) The magnetic relationship of the center.
4. Experiment on the part of the driver, in order that he may learn his business.
5. The formulatory center reporting the behavior of the organism to the "I".
6. Formulation of observations concurrent with the act of observation.
7. Formulation of ideas.
8. The attempt to understand the ideas.
9. The attempt to relate the ideas and understand the relationships.
10. The attempt to define terms in accordance with Institute ideas.
11. The attempt to interpret life, human beings, etc., in terms of mechanicality.
12. Describe experience I reflect on the ideas.
13. Triangulate, that is have a three-fold purpose for each act.
14. Assemble all you know of a given object at the moment of perceiving it.
15 . Constructive imagination
    (a) Image the great octave
    (b) Attempt to realize man's position in the universe.
16. Relate each object to its position in the scale. For instance, a cigarette belongs to the vegetable kingdom. The gold of a watch to

the metals (do). Man (si). Etc. The whole natural kingdom is interposed between (mi) and planets (fa) of the great octave. Etc.

17. Attempt to realize the fact of two thousand million people.

18. Attempt to realize the fact of death.

19. Be aware of the weight of an opinion

20. Apply the law of the octave to one's own behavior. Attempt to know when any given impulse has reached (mi).

21. Peel the onion, that is, make notations of the various attitudes toward life, stripping off the superficial ones in an effort to reach the fundamental attitude.

21. Note likes and dislikes.

22. Find the essential wish.

23. Find the chief feature.

24. Make gratuitous efforts.

25. Cast a role for oneself.

26. Pursue an impossible task.

27. Go against inclination.

28. Push inclination beyond the limits of its natural desire.

29. If a man force you to go one mile with him, go with him twain

30. Determine what it is you really want in any given situation. Deliberately get it, or deliberately oppose the "I" to this wish. At any event, non-identify with it, the wish.

31. Practice the mental gymnastics relative to time, space, and motion.

32. Seek for concrete illustrations and examples (in experience) of the ideas.

33. Try to perform, consciously, instinctive, emotional, and intellectual work at the same time.

34. Try to keep in mind that at any given moment you are actualizing one of several possibles [sic].

35. Try to keep in mind that when you talk these ideas to someone or to a group, human cells are at that moment instructing a group of monkey cells—within each brain.

36. Try to realize that man, oneself, is a cosmos. That this organism is the plane or globe of this "I". That it (the organism) contains cells corresponding to the categories of nature.

37. Try to become aware of the operations of sub-centers: the emotional and moving sub-centers of the intellectual, the intellectual and instinctive of the emotional, the intellectual and emotional sub-centers of the instinctive.

38. Try to keep in mind and realize that this organism is, in reality, a mere bubble. That is, in fact, the whole material or actualized universe is related to the potential universe as shadow is to substance.

[No 39]

40. Give all five points the necessary activity.

41. The attempt to use the formulatory center as a muscle, directly, and independent of sub-vocalizing.

42. The attempt to repeat a poem and a series of numbers, simultaneously, using the formulatory center for the poem, the vocalizing apparatus for the numbers.

43. Unroll the film.

44. Evoke in pictures the objects to which ideas are created.

45. Supply the base, the third force, the neutralizer, in all and every situation. That is, *improvise*.

46. Cast spells.

47. Try to practice conscious morality.

48. Try to think of the reasonable thing to do or say in any given situation.

49. Each event is potentially a complete circle. But circumstances usually distort it or at best, supply only a curve. If this much is supplied:

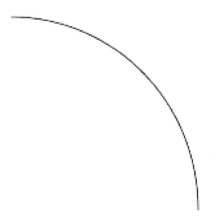

try to determine just what is reasonably necessity [sic] to complete it. Supply it, thus:

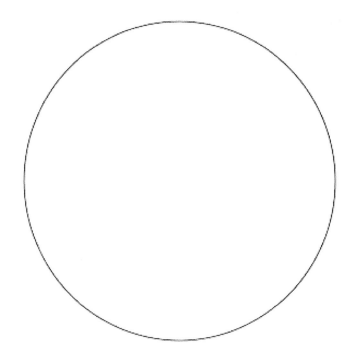

Chapter 2. Representative Works of Oragean Modernism

This chapter provides brief discussions of some representative works of Oragean Modernism. By giving some attention to the individual expressions of the writers it will be possible to arrive at a more comprehensive understanding of the movement. The works discussed are as follows:

Walter Gilkyson. *The Lost Adventurer* (1927).
Isa Glenn. *East of Eden* (1932).
John Dos Passos. *1919* (1932).
Marjorie Kinnan Rawlings. *South Moon Under* (1933).
John O'Hara. *Appointment in Samarra (*1934).
Dawn Powell. *Turn, Magic Wheel.* (1936).
Djuna Barnes. *Nightwood* (1936).
James Agee. *Let Us Now Praise Famous Men* [1936] (1941).
Marjorie Kinnan Rawlings. *The Yearling* (1938).
Ralph Ellison. *Invisible Man* (1952)

Walter Gilkyson. *The Lost Adventurer* **(1927).** Nobody remembers any of the books that Dashiel Hammet reviewed in 1927, observes LeRoy Panek (64), and Panek is right that *The Lost Adventurer* was lost to obscurity long ago. But as Hammet was *The Saturday Review*'s expert on mysteries, it is worth noting that he reviewed Gilkyson's novel as a mystery:

This is the story of Rann McCloud, young proprietor of a Pennsylvania newspaper in the 'sixties,' who championed the cause of the humble Ellises, lost his paper and his home in the resultant libel suit, married Isabel d'Alvarez, went with her to live in her Uncle Policarpo's Altean castle, became a major in the Spanish army, was jailed for Republican beliefs, escaped, was recaptured and ordered deported, and drowned while swimming ashore to see Isabel, who meanwhile and without his knowledge was traveling to join him aboard ship. The book's plan is ironical. Its execution is not. The result is confusing. Rann McCloud is not adventurous. He is a sullen young man of no great intelligence. His interests, like his hatreds, are picayune. Had he accomplished all the few things he attempted he still would have been a man of no importance. The greatest height he can achieve is an exhibition of that senseless obstinacy which is the courage of the very weak. Mr. Gilkyson seems to take this oaf seriously, to consider him an admirable figure. To himself Rann McCloud seems a giant. To his wife he seems a giant. That's all very well. But when Mr. Gilkyson agreed with them he spoiled his book. (*The Saturday Review*. June 11, 1927)

The Lost Adventurer is one of the Oragean Modernist's historical novels that Dawn Powell points to in *Turn, Magic Wheel*. Until I had realized what Powell was saying in her description of the publisher's library, it had not been possible to begin to search for these texts, since until then it seemed as though the output of Orage's school was confined to comic novels. At this point in assessing the literary output of Orage's school, Walter Gilkyson's historical novel may be placed in the company of Elinor Wylie's *Mr. Hodge & Mr. Hazard* and *The Orphan Angel*, Arna Bontemps *Black Thunder*, John Dos Passos's *USA*, and with Zora Neale Hurston's *Moses Man of the Mountain*. Other such esoteric historical novels will no doubt turn up as the membership of the school is added to. Like the other novels in this group,*The Lost Adventurer* is the account of the failed life of a flawed individual. We may see this as the problem of the Oragean Modernist brand, for the view of human action that is accorded by the Higher Learning tends to demonstrate that there is little more for an ordinary person to do that to "die like a dog": certainly Rann McCloud does little more than to make a series of horrible mistakes and then go to a meaningless death.

Reading *The Lost Adventurer* in the context of other Oragean Modernist novels makes visible the strangeness of many of the other works in this category; as in contrast to such works as *Nightwood* or *The Yearling* there is barely anything in Gilkyson's novel to alert the reader that the novel has an esoteric subtext. Often the very title of an Oragean Modernist novel poses a quandary, but there is nothing remarkable about *The Lost Adventurer.* There is little action and little consistency, so the text offers no possibilities for "lawful inexactitudes." Neither are the names of the characters overly suggestive. If some thought is applied, it soon comes into awareness that the name of the characters mimics the action of the character. The hero, Rann McCloud, is forced to leave his home town in Pennsylvania, and after relocating to Spain, his wife's native land, he is deported, and suffers an accidental death on the way to the boat that will take him back to America. His name tells us that he is repeatedly "run out" of places, so the novel confirms his accidental destiny. In other words, the novel explores the esoteric theme of the accidental life as opposed to the life of the "real man" that "can do." By the same token his wife is named Isabel d' Alvarez, meaning "all true": it is she who states that "He knows nothing of himself" (76). This is at once the theme of the novel, the "truth" for which d' Alvarez is named, and the esoteric principle that is expressed through Gilkyson's novel—for above all Gurdjieff taught that it is important to "know yourself" in order not "to die like a dog." It seems to Rann McCloud that it is the villain, Clarence Weir, who brings about his downfall, and though "Weir" is the name of a type of trap, it is McCloud who entraps himself. McCloud has a means of escape, but at the climax of his trial he chooses to suppress the evidence that he could have used to free himself. In the two main actions of the novel, it is McCloud's categorical mode of thought that brings him to ruin. Only when he is utterly without resources does he finally assume the disguise of a priest and make his escape. Having escaped, he then is determined to turn himself into the authorities, but since he returns to the castle of his wife's monarchist uncle he is captured and surrenders even that absurd degree of self-determination.

While there is use of the phonetic *cabala* throughout the novel, it is handled superficially, and the reader does not experience the destruction of the realism of the text that one sees in the novels of Van Vechten and others. Well into the text, Gilkyson inserts a passage that plays on the phonetic similarity of the word "nude" and Christian Newd's name:

> "Oh, Blicker!" Rann grinned, feeling sorry for him, and at the same time a little puzzled. "Tell me, what was bawdy and carnal in what I said?"
>
> "About Christian Newd runnin' naked after naked women," said Blicker promptly. "They was only references, I know but—" he shook his head—"I heard more than one person say they was bawdy an' carnal."
>
> "God!" Rann shot back in his chair. "You mean what I said about Christian Newd and the naked truth?" (80-1)

This play on Newd and nude presumably sets things up for A.R. Orage's name coded as "Ramsay's cigar store" in the following sentence: "Well, as long as God wasn't almighty angry about it yesterday down at Ramsay's cigar store, I don't much care,' Rann grunted, and Blicker shrank back aghast" (81). At many points in the text there seems to be the suggestion of names "grotesque gestures...mumblings and shufflings" (83) tending vaguely toward the presentation of "Gurdjieff", but they are of little help to the reader who is not already aware of what is intended by these effects.

Isa Glenn. *East of Eden* **(1932).** *East of Eden* is a *roman a clef* about Elinor Wylie, who in the novel is called Eva Litchfield. Elinor Morton Wylie (September 7, 1885 – December 16, 1928) was an American poet and novelist popular in the 1920s and 1930s. She was famous during her life almost as much for her ethereal beauty and personality as for her melodious, sensuous poetry. Glenn may have chosen the name Litchfield for Wylie because she believed that it meant "field of the dead." Wylie was a troubled personality, and her self-destructive tendencies brought her an early demise. It was recognized by her friends that she was in trouble, and her friends and fellow celebrity poet Edna St. Vincent

Millay tried to help her change her self-destructive habits of excessive alcohol consumption and fast living.

Wylie, according to Paul Beekman Taylor, "relied on Orage to help her renew her talent" (*Gurdjieff's American* 287). Since Glenn was a follower of Orage, one would think that Glenn's novel would be an account of Wylie's dealings with Orage, but this is not so. While Orage is present in the novel, he is called "the Englishman" and he remains in the background, discoursing about philosophy at parties while most of the revelers ignore him (9-13). The novel is confined to presenting those who gossip avidly about Eva Litchfield's marriage to the wealthy heir of a Manhattan real estate fortune, Nicholas Van Suydam. Curiously, it is through Eva Litchfield's mother-in-law that Gurdjieff comes into the novel, for he takes the part of her coach-driver, Higginson. The novel has the elderly Mrs. Van Suydam act out the "parable of the coach"—a key Gurdjieffian text; this parable was a motif used in several Oragean Modernist novels. Gurdjieff-Higginson, like Orage-the Englishman, remains a background character, and there is nothing on the surface of the novel that gives any indication that these two figures are of more than rudimentary importance. As a point of further confusion, Higginson's employer, Mrs. Van Suydam, is allowed to voice esoteric ideas that derive from Orage: she observes that "It is a disease, this writing of books" (26). Since *East of Eden* primarily concerns the literary celebrity of Eva Litchfield, Mrs. Van Suydam's opinion effectively frames the theme of the novel—that Eva Litchfield is diseased. Louise Welch summarizes Orage's approach to literature as flowing from disease as follows:

> Orage maintained that the style was the man. To us it meant that if we read perceptively, we would penetrate a writer's gifts and weaknesses. It is interesting now to see how often he hit the nail on the head, for nowadays, when biographers spare nobody literary candor, we can verify Orage's opinion of a writer's abnormality, physical or psychological. One writer, who, from his style Orage diagnosed as syphilitic, is now known to

have had the disease. Another who suffered from a diarrhea of words had the organic difficulty as well, and several whose rhythms gave away their homosexuality have since confessed, or boasted, if it. Orage's insight was never a judgment but an acute perception of illness through style. Study manifestation, he said, and you will know who another is— even who you yourself are. (Welch 63)

The names of Glenn's characters are expressed as clichés through the phonetic *cabala*: the narrator, Dinah Avery is "very handy." The other names are coded in the same manner: Spencer Mapes / ape man, Jamus Pomeroy / jump for joy, Justo Zermonte / just monstrous, Gertrude Cuyler / cruel truth, Anthony Bloodgood / bloody good thing, Winnie Conant [Fania Marinoff] / constant whining, Charles Glidden / gladdened heart, and Nicholas Van Suydam / damn you. The names coded in the phonetic *cabala* served as the key by which the esoteric level of the novel was to be accessed. Presenting more difficulty, since the names of the esoteric teachers are not familiar, the novel uses the phonetic *cabala* to present the names of Gurdjieff ("...higgledy-piggeldy. Work is out, darling!" [60]), Orage ("outrageous devil" [25]), and Ouspensky ("gushingly...point" [3]—i.e., gush-point-ly). The text also presents a smattering of the Gurdjieffian terms and ideas— work (18); the parable of the coach (20, 101-2); the Moon (21); possibilities (64); and superhuman effort (64).

The novel was reviewed by Carl Van Doren, and as Van Doren's assessment makes a number of valuable points, I will reproduce the review in its entirety below:

Eva Litchfield's story, of course, has no actual resemblance to Elinor Wylie's. The one likeness between the two women is in the abstract conception of their aloofness and ambition. If Elinor Wylie had had no traits but these, and if she had married a man like Nicholas Van Suydam with a mother like his, she might then have become an Eva Litchfield. She would, however, not have been Elinor Wylie. And she would never, vivid as she always was, racy as she could be, have been the wraith of a genius, the unvisualized, half-spectral girl that Eva Litchfield is in "East of Eden." The book is what it claims to be: the story of Eva Litchfield. It is not what it is said to be: the story of Elinor Wylie. I stress the distinction as with a crowbar because the novel is bound to be read by people hunting for what is not there. Some of them will find just enough lifelike details, particularly as regards the incidental characters, to convince them that Eva Litchfield is lifelike too. The visiting Englishman unmistakably suggests Ford Madox Ford, as Daniel Pentreath no less unmistakably suggests Robert Chanler. Molly Underhill owes something to Dorothy Parker, Dinah Avery to Isa Glenn. The Onion Party given by Winnie Conant for women only recalls the historical event arranged by Fania Marinoff. Several of the interiors have been reported from actual houses rather than invented. The list could be prolonged. Yet the points of resemblance are dexterously shuffled. Winnie Conant and her husband Addis Wickersham are extremely unlike Fania Marinoff and Carl Van Vechten. Florence Quincy appears to be a synthesis. The characterization of the man here called Lucullus Kahn—"a faun with fleas"—was in fact first hit upon, I understand, by a different person on a different occasion. This list also could be prolonged. But the total of veracity in the book may be misleading as to Elinor Wylie. (*The Saturday Review.* October 15, 1932. 173.)

Van Doren's review shows that *East of Eden* is not a realistic portrait of the people that it presents, since he cannot recognize Wylie, Van Vechten, and Fania Marinoff. In contrast to his normally ebullient personality, Glenn's version of Carl Van Vechten shows him to be forbidding and remote:

Addis Wickersham lingered behind the table on which he continued to mix drinks for his wife's woman-party. He mixed the drinks automatically his eyes fixed and glassy, staring at no woman in particular but surprised by all, shuddering at no one incident but revolted by the sum total of womankind in the raw. He murmured, as if to his secret locked-away mind: "What a ghastly sight—a lot of women stuffing onions down their gullets!" Onions disagreed with him. He continued, however, in a spirit of masochism, to stare at the party, and his occasional shudders rippled unperceived over the immaculate surface of his pose. It was with what appeared to be amusement that he called out to his wife: "Winfreda, my spouse, this is intolerable!" (191-92)

This shift away from reality discloses the shape that Glenn's esoteric novel brings to actual events and personalities. The reason for this alteration is that the theme of Glenn's novel is the idea that the root cause of the disease of the writer mentioned above is "false personality." The Onion Party to which Van Doren refers was a real event that was recast in the novel to deliver an esoteric content. The onion was, like the overcoat [see my discussion of *Miss Lonelyhearts*], a reification of the idea of false personality. The overcoat and the onion represented the layers of false personality:

> Our personality is made up of a false personality, which is concerned with our ego (pride, vanity, self-conceit, imaginations and day-dreams about ourselves, etc.), and personality proper, which is developed through education, vocation, training and study of all kinds, and which enables us to earn our living.
>
> The source of our fundamental self or REAL I, is our essence. In primitive peoples, and people who live close to Nature or who do creative work, it is often less smothered by the false personality, but its development is still usually limited. (Benjamin *Gurdjieff's System*)

Glenn's description of Wickersham is deceptive and needs to be unpacked. The automatic manner in which he mixes the drinks is not a real attribute, it is a mask. Behind the mask he reserves his "secret locked-away mind" (192). Wickersham seems to banter with the women, but his speeches have a double meaning. The women are not taking off the layers of their onions, their false personalities; they are instead *eating* the onions—in effect they are internalizing their false personalities. The opera star (Georgette Leblanc) declares that the onions are good for the larynx, and Wickersham replies, "Your own larynx is a fine one, Madame. I saw it distinctly." (192). Wickersham indicates that he has looked *within* the opera star and that he has ascertained the degree of degeneration and disease in her being. Addis Wickersham is phonetic *cabala* for "What a shame." Similarly, the visiting Englishman, who Van Doren names as Ford Madox Ford, is A.R. Orage: the Englishman asks, "Do you know how to live?" (137). The Englishman's question is in keeping with the topics that were pursued at Orage's meetings. Glenn's novel narrowly pursues Orage's question of how must life be lived, with the answer a foregone conclusion. Eva Litchfield does not know how to live. She misses every opportunity to save herself; and she goes to an unfortunate death.

John Dos Passos. *1919* **(1932).** John Dos Passos attended the New York performances of Gurdjieff's dance troupe in 1924 and was a regular at Orage's lectures. Since the occult does not enter into the discussion of the Lost Generation, and since Dos Passos's leftist activities dominate discussions of his novels and of his career, the definitive picture of him is very different from what his writings contain. What is of particular importance in this discussion is the establishment of Dos Passos's importance at the time his novels were published, since what I want to emphasize is the cultural centrality achieved by the Oragean Modernist literary movement. As the passage below shows, Dos Passos had achieved great literary importance before he was demoted by the "red scare":

One hundred years after his birth, Dos Passos is an anomaly: his fictions of the 1920's and 1930's, *Three Soldiers* (1921), *Manhattan Transfer* (1925), and the trilogy *U.S.A.* (1930—1936, 1937) are acknowledged to be important works in American literary history. He is regularly anthologized; but rarely is he eulogized, a far cry from his situation in 1936, when he was featured on the cover of the August 10th issue of *Time* magazine to mark the publication of *The Big Money,* the third volume of *U.S.A.* Two years later Jean-Paul Sartre acclaimed him "the greatest living writer of our time." (Luddington "John Dos Passos")

Given the chronological spread of his published writing, we would not expect to see that Dos Passos would have been writing esoteric novels until he had reached the *U.S.A.* trilogy. In *Manhattan Transfer* there is a typical piece of esoteric business at the commencement of the novel. Dos Passos allows the word "leg" suffice to indicate that a "legominism" will follow each use of "leg":

Just as the band passed the Commanding General his horse stood upon his hind *legs* and was almost erect. General Miles instantly reined in the frightened animal and dug in his spurs in an endeavor to control the horse which to the horror of the spectators, fell over backwards and landed squarely on the Commanding General. Much to the gratification of the people General Miles was not injured but considerable *skin* was scraped off the flank of the horse. Almost every inch of General Miles's overcoat was covered with the *dust* of the street and between the shoulders a hole about an inch in diameter was *punctured.* Without waiting for anyone to brush the dust from his garments General Miles remounted his horse and reviewed the parade as if it were an everyday occurrence. (3; emphasis added)

The "legominism" that follows the use of "leg" is the name of Ouspensky given by the words *dust-punctured-skin.* This usage obtains throughout the novels of the trilogy. By means of this device Dos Passos alludes to the beginning course of the Oragean Version of the Hidden Teaching through the actions that his characters carry out. Joe Williams's incarceration refers to the idea that man is in prison and does not know it. The imprisonment theme is brought into Rawlings's novel through characterization: the mad raftsman's name, Ramrod Simpson, itself delivers the idea–"[I] am [a] prisoner." But in *1919* Dos Passos presents the ideas through action, not through *allusive character- symbolism.* Since the signaling for the *legominism* is even vaguer in *1919* than in *South Moon Under,* there is little chance that Dos Passos' reader will even hesitate over the esoteric material unless they wonder that anyone can be as stupid as Joe Williams: the question then is as to whether Joe Williams the character serves as a "lawful inexactitude" that might alert the reader that all is not right in the novel.

Again, when Williams encounters a homosexual who tries to pick him up, the episode exhibits the operation of the formatory apparatus:

> He talked a 'blue streak' all the time they were driving out past the British bungalows and brick institution buildings and after that out along the road through rubbery blue woods so dense and steamy it seemed to Joe there must be a glass roof overhead somewhere. He said how he liked adventure and travel and wished he was free to ship on boats and bum around and see the world and that it must be wonderful to depend only on your own sweat and muscle the way Joe was doing. (640-41)

The homosexual talks "a blue streak" because he is mechanical and his formatory apparatus is in control of his actions:

The mechanical part of the intellectual center has a special name: it is called the formatory apparatus, because, in the right functioning of the human machine, it is intended to set up forms for the higher parts of the center to operate upon.

In man as he is, the formatory apparatus has run wild and dominates psychic life. Its constant din of associations makes it almost impossible for a man to become quiet and observe himself as he is.

Because modern life is filled with formatory associations, even man number one and number two are often far from direct experience of their bodies and feelings. Consequently, a very important place in the Work is occupied by attention to the sensation of the body. This sensation is a stable point which can be of great help in developing sustained self-remembering. (Langdon "Gurdjieff's Ideas")

What the homosexual says testifies to the poor relationship that he has with his surroundings—a feature of the operation of the formatory apparatus—and the homosexual is allowed to say as much about himself, though without any realization of the meaning of his words.

At times Dos Passos constructs a "legominism" that has a bearing on the organization of the school. In one passage, the school is presented as a ship on which Joe Williams has a posting:

"He said he'd have a berth for Joe as junior officer on the Henry B. Higginbotham as soon as she'd finished repairs and he must go to work at shore school over in Norfolk and get ready to go before the licensing board and get his ticket" (705).

Like other Oragean Modernist authors, Dos Passos uses words with "igg" and "iggi" to indicate George Ivanovich Gurdjieff's name. However, the ship is not so much the man as his school. In the narrative the Higginbotham sinks and the captain dies of pneumonia. The next action presents a good deal of ambiguity on the esoteric level of the text:

> Next morning Joe and the mate went to the office of the agent of Perkins and Ellerman, the owners, to see about getting themselves and the crew paid off. There was some kind of damn monkeydoodle business about the vessel's having changed owners in midAtlantic, a man named Rosenberg had bought her on a speculation and now he couldn't be found and the Chase National Bank was claiming ownership and the underwriters were raising cain. (829)

Perkins and Ellerman, the name of the original owners, is phonetic *cabala* for Maxwell Perkins. The new owner, Rosenberg, seems to be Paul Rosenberg, the French art dealer. When Orage left New York and then died in 1931, the New York school was returned to the direction of Gurdjieff. This arrangement seems to be alluded to by the transfer of the school from Maxwell Perkins, a New Yorker, to Paul Rosenberg, a resident of Paris. The events are clouded by the fact that in the narrative the ship—which carries Gurdjieff's name— is sunk, so in effect this says that the New York school does not so much transfer back to Gurdjieff as disappear. Additionally, we learn that the crew does not get paid, so is in an unresolved difficulty: as the first mate says to the clerk—"And what the hell do they expect us to do all that time, eat grass?" (829-30). Williams ships out and gets into trouble on a Caribbean island, when he is saved by a stranger:

> They were in the middle of a yelling bunch of big black men when they heard an American voice behind them, "Don't say another word, boys, I'll handle this." A small man in khaki riding breeches and a panama hat was pushing his way through the crowd talking in the island lingo all the time. He was a little man with a gray

triangular face tufted with a goatee. "My name's Henderson, DeBuque Henderson of Bridgeport, Connecticut," He shook hands with both of them. (832)

DeBuque Henderson is phonetic *cabala* for "book of understanding" and refers to *The Oragean Version* which continues to be circulated in Work circles today. "Bridgeport" gives the name "Orage" in *cabala*. The exaggerated description of the house is saturated with esoteric ideas. The description emphasizes the words "light" and "lighter;" the word "working" is a combination of work and king—indicating the Gurdjieff Work and C. Daly King in one word. The word "interval" is an important contribution from the esoteric vocabulary: the interval accounts for the idea that eventually everything becomes its opposite—as Ouspensky points out: The "intervals" cause the line of the development of force to constantly change. Think how many turns the line of development of forces must have taken to come from the Gospel preaching of love to the Inquisition (Ouspensky *Search* 129).

> When they got to his house he walked them through a big whitewashed room onto a terrace that smelt of vanilla flowers. They could see the town underneath with its few *lights*, the dark hills, the white hull of the Callao with the *lighters* around her lit up by the *working lights*. At intervals the rattle of winches came up to them and a crazy jigtune from somewhere. (833; emphasis added)

The description is an allusion to a specific passage in *The Oragean Version*:

> It is the task of an objective physics to distinguish accurately between all these, and particularly in respect of their different vibration-rates, the higher the vibration-rate the lighter and more vivified the matter, the lower the rate the denser, heavier, slower and less vivified the matter. It is a corollary of this view that the Universe is both living and *growing*, in contradistinction to the

scientific implication, sometimes plainly stated, that it is mostly dead and in other respects dying in accordance with the so-called second law of thermodynamics. (*Oragean Version* 197)

As a further identification of Henderson with Orage, Dos Passos has Henderson tell the sailors that United Fruit is a monopoly. Here "monopoly" is a reference to Orage's dedication to C. H. Douglas's interdisciplinary distributive philosophy called Social Credit; Douglas was the author of a book titled *The Monopoly of Credit* to which the passage alludes.

Marjorie Kinnan Rawlings. *South Moon Under* **(1933).** Though it has not previously been part of Rawlings's biography, it is apparent from reading the novel that Rawlings was one of A.R. Orage's followers. *South Moon Under* is an allegorical treatment of Gurdjieff's teachings about the Moon. If the title is read by phonetic *cabala* it says "Earth soon doomed." The Oragean Modernists believed that the agent of the Earth's destruction was the Moon. The heroic pace at which literary texts were produced by the Oragean Modernists was motivated by their belief that the destruction of the Earth was imminent and that only super-efforts by the few people on the Earth who were not "asleep" would allow the planet to be saved. *The Oragean Version* discusses the Moon-Earth relationship as follows:

Mankind on this planet is not the entire human race for, if so, we could never have known a Buddha or a Christ, by their own original accounts messengers not from heaven but from elsewhere in this universe. And just as the sheep could see the shepherd well enough but did not understand at all what he was, so we can, and do, see our shepherd almost every day without the slightest recognition of his real role in our lives. He is not an abstraction nor is he a generality; he is no such thing as Nature in general or Nature with a capital N, he is a specific and concrete part of Nature. For men on this planet their shepherd is the Moon. And because the Moon is specific to this planet, the black sheep's secret is specific to this planet, too. It will not do, however, to consider the Moon as a kind of devil. Devils are no more than the inventions of romanticists and there are no authentic devils in this universe, although it is true that Nature may properly be called our Evil Stepmother. In a perfectly proper sense it is Nature which exiles man from his high destiny and keeps him in his exile. Nature here is to be considered in her most general aspects, not only in those aspects of man's own nature which continually prevent his awakening from his usual semiconscious state but also in those aspects of the mechanicality and automatism. The immediate manifestation of the latter aspects for us upon the Earth is man's Bad Shepherd, the Moon. (60-61)

The oppressive atmosphere of *South Moon Under* is in keeping with the above passage. Given the strangeness and unfamiliarity of the teachings recorded in *The Oragean Version*, I think that it is useful to quote additionally from C. Daly King's rendering of Orage's discussion of the Moon:

This interposition of Organic Kingdoms between the given constituent elements or given successive cosmic levels of the Universe is also necessary to the universal feeding process of the whole. For there is a reciprocal, very complicated process of that kind which continually goes forward throughout the entire Universe, keeping it in a perpetual balance and activity; it applies not only within the limits of an Organic Kingdom, within which a delicate balance is maintained among the various species which are the naturally respective prey of each other, but a comparable sort of reciprocal feeding is instituted throughout the whole manifested Reality. The Earth, as we know, is not overrun by certain insects for this very reason; in Bermuda, for instance, the ants are eaten by the cockroaches and the cockroaches are eaten by the spiders; and in any locality, when these balances are upset (usually by some artifice of the ignorance or of the meddling of semiconscious man), very serious results ensue, such as crop failures due to a sudden outbreak of pest propagation or to some unexpected increase in soil erosion, and so on. Such balances, however, are not confined only to the phenomena of Organic Kingdoms and they pervade and maintain the operation of the full universal economy. Often we do not see the ends of these trains of reciprocal feeding in either direction and assume erroneously that they are both more circumscribed and local than they are. In our own case much of the Earth's Organic Kingdom feeds man directly or indirectly. Man in turn feeds the Moon, as well as enriching the planet's soil by his body's inevitable decay.

These are the real, objective functions which man serves in the economy of Nature whether he knows it or not, these transformations of cosmic energies through his own life process and, at its conclusion, the passing on of such accumulated and transformed energies, which are drawn toward the Moon automatically at his death. There is nothing too astounding in the situation, for is has long been known, by perfectly ordinary means, that the human organism is primarily a device for the transformation of what are called electrical energies. The fuller information, however, cannot but effect a radical alteration in our customary values, especially as concerns those extraordinary persons often called geniuses, psychics, and those endowed with what are supposed to be great and remarkable talents. For the more extraordinary such persons may be considered, the more are they *ipso facto* the more valuable slaves of the Moon, it being plain that the greater the amount of energies down-graded in these more complex nervous systems during lifetime the richer is the energy-supply projected toward the satellite at their deaths, as compared with the cases of ordinary people. This is one, but only one, of the reasons for which it is said in this Version that the path to development is from the extraordinary through the ordinary to the normal. If one has the misfortune to be "an extraordinary man", then first he must become ordinary before an opportunity is at all open too him to become normal. It is neither mere superstition nor mere ignorance which has given the Moon's name, in an objective sense, to lunatics.

For the Moon is the real mainspring of human activity on this planet, it is the great pendulum imparting motion to all the doings of semiconscious men. Their greatest heroisms and their greatest crimes are equally the outcome of their lunar-motivated sleep. That they are asleep is yet to be shown, and literally so; but that shall come at its proper place in the narrative. This is the Actual about men as regards Cosmogony, that though unwittingly they are nonetheless objectively the mechanical slaves of the Moon. Not only so but the more powerful the dictator, the more fanatic and successful the religionist, the more renowned the philosopher, the more celebrated the mathematical genius; by this very token the more is he the Moon's slave. (63-4)

In Rawlings's novel this idea is expressed lyrically but with some ambiguity, since Lant is not an initiate of esotericism and so is not able to formulate the idea that the Moon is the actual cause of his difficulties with any surety:

South moon was under. On the other side of the earth the moon rode high, and it had power to move the owls and rabbits. He closed his eyes and listened in the darkness to the rhythmic call. He wondered if it might be so with men. Perhaps all men were moved against their will. A man ordered his life, and then an obscurity of circumstance sent him down a road that was not of his own desire or choosing. Something beyond a man's immediate choice and will reached through the earth and stirred him. He did not see how any man might escape it.

Neither river nor swamp nor hammock nor impenetrable scrub could save a man from the ultimate interference. There was no safety. There was no retreat. Forces beyond his control, beyond his sight and hearing, took him in their vast senseless hands when they were ready. The whole earth must move as the sun and moon and an obscure law directed—even the earth, planet-ridden and tormented. (Chapter 34)

The Moon is described as a regulating instrument in *South Moon Under*: in the passage above it is presented as a fact that the residents of the scrub are able to perceive the position of the Moon at any time of the day. Additionally, it is established that "Paine had passed on to the boy his lore of scrub and hammock," so that Lant knows that "the deer feeds on the moon, like most ary wild creeter. Four times the deer feeds. Stirs or feeds. Moon-rise and moon-down, and south-moon-over and south-moon-under" (Chapter XI). The two propositions that (1) it is possible to know the movements of the Moon as it moves around the Earth and (2) that "the deer feeds on the moon" are run together, so that it seems as though these conditions are joined. The idea as it is presented suggests that if hunters can act on these actualities they are better able to bring down game and to feed themselves: the corollary also suggests that if these conditions are not followed they will starve to death.

I have consulted with Dr. Judith S. Young of the Department of Astronomy at the University of Massachusetts, Amherst, who is an expert on the movements of the Moon. In commenting on the information in *South Moon Under*, Dr. Young points out that given the complexity of the factors that are involved it is not possible to know the daily movements of the Moon unless one is an advanced astronomer, thus the lore presented by Rawlings in her novel is fictional. The phases of the Moon that are commonly noticed are the monthly phases, and this is not at all what is meant by "south-moon-over and south-moon-under," which are daily movements. The question as to whether Rawlings invented the "south-moon-over and south-moon-under" terminology has not been resolved as yet, though no source other than Rawlings's novel has been discovered. It seems unlikely that Rawlings heard this from the Florida natives since it is impossible for them to be speaking about these occurrences. Admittedly, the natives are said to feel the position of the Moon, not to calculate it. As for the idea that "the deer feeds on the moon" this is a different sort of problem: the esoteric idea—as stated in the quote from *The Oragean Version* above—is that "Man in turn feeds the Moon," so it would seem that here Rawlings has inserted a "lawful inexactitude" about "food" to compliment the initial "lawful inexactitude" (a discrepancy used to indicate the presence of a hidden content) about knowing the movements of the Moon. It is not important whether or not deer actually regulate their activities according to the position of the Moon, since the original "south-moon-over and south-moon-under" proposition is specious. In other words, the entire treatment of the Moon in *South Moon Under* is esoteric and all of the seemingly documentary aspects of the presentation of this information that Rawlings gives to the lore about the Moon is contrived to set up absurdities that will ultimately reveal the presence of esoteric information. Unfortunately, these absurdities have been taken at face value and their fictiveness has not been discovered by her critics.

We may speak of the process of liberation from sleep and mechanicality as alchemy, for in essence that is the nature of the Oragean Modernist endeavor, and indeed the Oragean Modernists thought of themselves as spiritual alchemists. Alchemy was given literary expression in the Oragean Modernist's texts. Tolson's *Harlem Gallery* is replete with alchemical lore and the names of many alchemists; Thurman's novel, *Infants*, contains a veiled description of an alchemical laboratory (see Woodson 57); and Barnes's *Nightwood* forthrightly flaunts the word "alchemy" (83).

There are two manifestations of alchemy in the Rawlings's novels —language and moonshining.

In all of the Oragean Modernist novels a code is used to hide the esoteric content. This code is the traditional code of the alchemists; it is a phonetic code that is nearly impossible for normal readers to deal with, since normal readers do not read by applying phonetic variability so that vowels and syllables are adjusted to allow for a meaning to be arrived at. This alchemical code runs interminably so that at any point in the text one can register names appearing in some manner. In order to give some idea of the intricacy of Rawlings's use of phonetic *cabala* I will present a particularly dense and complexly allusive passage where the Jacklin family is desperately hunting for food:

> The trail led into the rough, a patch of ground that had been lately burned, and the fire put out by rains. The area here was as the scrub had been in front of Lantry's clearing when he first moved from across the river. The new growth was low and tangled, matted with stumps and burned trees. Because the strip was narrow, the three continued across it. It lead into old scrub; scrub whose tall pines were bent by the storm of '71. The pines grew openly, with stretches carpeted with coarse grass, dotted with the grey-green of sweet myrtle bushes, of rosemary and sea-myrtle.
> The doe and fawn were here, bedding. The doe leaped up ahead of them. The fawn lurched to its feet and turned immense wondering eyes. Piety cocked her gun and levelled it; exerted her strength to pull the stiff trigger. She was slow. The fawn and doe were gone.
> The child went into a rage. He stamped his foot on the ground like an infuriated bull yearling. He spat, as he had seen Lantry do. His red-brown eyes glared at his mother. He seized the heavy gun from her hands and tried to put it to his shoulder to fire in the direction of the deer's retreat. He could not lift it. He stared at it. His fury subsided as quickly as it had come. (Chapter 7)

The setting is given by mentioning a storm. *Orage* is the French word for storm, and Orage comes in through the child's "rage" as well as "coarse," "lurched," and "fury," and the initials A.R. are suggested by a running series of words with "ar" in them —"narrow," "clearing," "yearling," "rosemary," "carpeted," etc. The storm took place in "'71," so that there is a clear allusion to the "Law of Seven." There are other references to the storm of '71 in the novel, where the storms are accompanied by the esoteric numbers 7 and 3 as in "I mind me. The big storm from the northeast. Hit blowed for three days and hit rained and purely loosened the roots" (Chapter 13). In Chapter 16 a storm clears after three days and then there is a discussion of "orange" trees—so the connection between storms, oranges, and the esoteric numbers 3 and 7 is made. In Chapter 18 a reference to a storm is connected to "work," so the undercurrent of reference to the esoteric is present with yet another variation. Thus the many storms in the novel are a recurring device that is intended to point to A.R. Orage. The name Ouspensky runs throughout the first paragraph—"as," "across," "pines," "pines," "openly," "trees," "three." Gurdjieff is suggested by "trigger." After reviewing these esoteric special effects, it is difficult to see this passage endowed with its former realism: the passage dissolves into an artificial construct, and the actions give way to an appearance of superficial contrivance.

Even when alerted to this code, it is difficult for the normal reader to handle the decoding. It also seems that the code is paradoxical, since the reader needs to know what is being said in order to determine the hidden content. However, since Rawlings provides the Gurdjieffian doctrine of the Moon's influence near the conclusion of the novel, there is some help in the novel towards understanding what is being imparted in the hidden levels. Rawlings's approach to the code is comparatively minimalist compared to Zora Neale Hurston's novels, and she is more like John O'Hara in that her names are tied to the way her characters are presented. Rawlings uses the names of her characters as clues to the way the phonetic code must be read. For instance, Cleve (C-leve) is her way of writing "evil." And Cleve it follows is an evil character. Cleve's evil is associated with the Moon, for Cleve looks white, round, and pasty. As I pointed out above, no one is going to read Cleve as "evil," since the normal way of reading is to consider the order of the letters always in one direction and "leve" must be reversed to arrive at "evil." And—since no one reads one letter as indicating another—"evel" is not easily understood as "evil." And then there is the issue of the extra letters that must be ignored when necessary: once this arrangement is understood, it is habit that prevents the alerted reader from making out the more difficult combinations. At the same time, Rawlings tries to instruct the reader: she uses the names Jim and Martin Posey to show that the "m" and the "n" are equivalent letters—for both names, Jim Posey and Martin Posey, deliver the coded word "impose." Kezzy and Zeke seem to be an attempt to teach the reader the idea that letters do not have to be in the expected order to make the word "key"— ignoring the z and reading phonetically: key (Kezzy) and kee (Zeke). Interestingly, in letters to Maxwell Perkins written while she was writing *South Moon Under* Rawlings referred to Kezzy as Kizzy, so one must wonder why the change was made other than to supply a "key" for the *cabala*.

Here are the names of some characters decoded:

Lantry Jacklin [Jack O'Lantern]
Ramrod Simpson [I am in prison]
Piety Lantry [Pity]
Moody (house) [doom]
Zeke / Kezzy [key]
Cleve Jacklin [evil]

The making of moonshine parallels the "art" of the spiritual alchemists—whose retort resembles the moonshiner's "outfit," as Rawlings refers to the moonshiner's still. The alchemist uses the still to achieve enlightenment, which is referred to in alchemy as The Stone. The Stone gives immortality. Whiskey (*usquebaugh*) is itself a word meaning "water of life." The moonshiners are so close to the alchemists in both their equipment and their products, immortality and "water of life," that there is a seamless fit between the literal and esoteric levels of the novel. In *South Moon Under* the process of the Moon feeding on men is reified when Cleve, the moon's vampire, goes about stealing the "water of life" from the moonshiners, the symbol of spiritual knowledge and immortality.

On the surface level the novel is beautifully written, and only towards the end does the esoteric material tend to take over and disturb the progress of the narrative. Since the novel is not about the creation of the superman, Lant is plunged suddenly into confusion. His name is actually Jack O' Lantern, and this indicates that he has a light within. In the early chapters he is admirable, moral, and possesses many talents. Toward the end he cannot see the truth any more. His world seems to be collapsing, and one of the topics of discussion of the denizens of the Scrub is how to live and how to restore their world. Read literally, the novel suffers from the esoteric message that the world can be saved through the esoteric Work. But as a one-dimensional novel, there seems to be a conflict between the levels that comes into play and makes the end less than satisfying. Lant suddenly falls apart and he can't even decide how to get rid of Cleve's body. Of course, since we do not know how to rid the world of Evil, this makes sense on the allegorical level. But it is an absurdity that Lant, who lives in a trackless wasteland and is an experienced woodsman, cannot find a satisfactory way to dispose of a dead body. The whole matter of Lant's absurd difficulty with Cleve's dead body is another "lawful inexactitude"—and it points to the esoteric law of evolution in the teachings about *reciprocal maintenance*—the inescapable relationship between food and cosmic life.

In *South Moon Under* Rawlings specifically addressed the fall of civilization that the Oragean Modernist looked to in the future. As in many of the Oragean Modernist texts, there is some ambiguity on this point as to what the downfall would look like. For instance, in Hurston's novels there is the suggestion that in the event of the failure of mankind another species might rise to the level of civilization. Gurdjieff's amanuensis, P.D. Ouspensky (See *In Search of the Miraculous*), records Gurdjieff's suggestion that ants and bees were once more highly evolved and were of a vastly greater size but were reduced when they failed to provide the needed spiritual food for the next level of life. Similarly, the fall of man will come about through the failure of the impulse to evolve:

> In theory, all tetartocosmoses can be vehicles by which Endlessness can know itself. Gurdjieff remarked that the ants and the bees were failed experiments in this respect, because they developed societies that were overwhelmingly mechanical and therefore impossible of self-consciousness. Gurdjieff saw mankind as an experiment in progress. To the extent that mankind remains mechanical, it will also be a failed experiment. To the extent that a sufficient number of human beings can become sufficiently self-conscious and therefore know the answer to the questions, who am I and what is the purpose of human life, the experiment succeeds. (Ginsburg *Gurdjieff Unveiled*)

Lant is thinking desperately about his failure to destroy Cleve's body and says, "The law's like to come up with me yet" (Chapter 35). Lant seems to be talking about civil law punishing him for murder, but he is also speaking of cosmic law. Because of the failure to evolve, man will be destroyed and replaced as the Moon's provider of food. These doctrines are suggested by the final image of the novel where Kezzy has her children look up at a mother cat-squirrel on a branch above their boat. The implication is that the cat-squirrels will replace the human race.

Despite the importance of the theme of doom in the novel, there is a counterbalance struck in the text by the esoteric operation of the "legominisms" that run through the text. One use for the "legominisms" is to preserve the esoteric teachings in the event that civilization suffers a catastrophe. While some Oragean Modernist texts give short shrift to this component of the esoteric novel, *South Moon Under* is a veritable esoteric encyclopedia. There are forty-three (43) uses of the word "leg" in the text. Each appearance of the word is followed by esoteric information. The first use of "leg" is followed by the notion that it is one thing to know and another to see. The principle here cast into folk wisdom has been given a deceptive simplicity. What Rawlings addresses is the idea that there is a difference between knowing and understanding:

> Towards the end of [*Beelzebub's Tales*], in the chapter "Form and Sequence," Gurdjieff draws a distinction between knowing and understanding. Understanding can only result through the conscious verification of knowledge. So, although the book presents knowledge, and perhaps knowledge of a very high order, it is not in itself useful unless one puts it to the test—digests it and converts it into understanding. (Owens "Commentary")

Subsequent "legominisms" introduced by the word "leg" address the major esoteric concepts of the Gurdjieff Work: sleep, unwinding the film, two kinds of notes, and they present the names of the teachers—Gurdjieff, Ouspensky.

Nathaniel West. *Miss Lonelyhearts* (1931). Nathaniel West's novel is an intricately fulfilled esoteric design, perhaps the most elaborate and successful of the Oragean Modernist canon. The text contains eight "legominisms" that are indicated by the word legominism presented in phonetic *cabala*: legs-man's; college, boot-legger, stiff-legged-"Armenian-like argument;" legs-lemon; college-men; legs-woman; "leg man;" leg, leg, money, man; legs-man [the phrases in quotation marks are as they are found in the text; the other presentations of "legominism" have words in between the component words]. Following each appearance of "leg" West inserted an esoteric idea, though in an unrecognizable form. For instance, in the first instance Shrike reads an absurd account of a religion that uses adding machines, and the article refers to *numbers as a universal language*. This is an allusion to the enneagram, a symbol that often appears in Gurdjieffian materials:

"Speaking in general it must be understood that the enneagram is a universal symbol. All knowledge can be included in the enneagram and with the help of the enneagram it can be interpreted. And in this connection only what a man is able to put into the enneagram does he actually know, that is, understand. What he cannot put into the enneagram he does not understand. For the man who is able to make use of it, the enneagram makes books and libraries entirely unnecessary. Everything can be included and read in the enneagram. A man may be quite alone in the desert and he can trace the enneagram in the sand and in it read the eternal laws of the universe. And every time he can learn something new, something he did not know before." (Ouspensky 301)

West's novel tells the story of a newspaper journalist who is assigned to write the "agony column." West was not a journalist, but in the 1920s A.R. Orage's associate Louise Michel Blinken Welch wrote such a column for the New York American. West has inserted Louise Michel's name at the beginning of his text using the phonetic *cabala*:

On his desk were piled those he had received this morning. He started through them again, searching for some *clue* to a sincere answer.

Dear *Miss* Lonelyhearts--

I am in such pain I dont know what to do sometimes I think I will *kill myself my* kidneys hurt so much. ("Miss Lonelyhearts, Help Me, Help Me"; emphasis added)

The name "Louise Michel" is somewhat indistinct, as are all of West's uses of phonetic *cabala*; the doubling of "my" is used as an aid—a common device—, and the name "Michel" must be read in reverse. "Louise" is delivered by "lue-iss"—out of "clue" and "Miss." That West bothers to identify the model for his protagonist is extraordinary, and a similar concern with external veracity characterizes West's treatment of the esoteric level of his novel. Like the other Oragean Modernist novelists, West constructs the names of his characters out of clichés, familiar phrases—in a reach for familiarity—, or of esoteric ideas. Ned Gates accompanies Miss Lonelyhearts on one of his drunken rampages through the city; which may be why he "gets [the] nod." But West is also more resourceful in his naming, and some of his names are directly allusive, so that they need to be defined in reference books. The feature editor, Shrike, is named for the butcherbird—any songbird of the chiefly Old World family *Laniidae,* having a heavy hooked bill and feeding on smaller animals which they sometimes impale on thorns or barbed wire. Thus Shrike's name may be taken literally, for he pinion's Miss Lonelyhearts on the job of answering the letters, just as the bird impales its prey. While Shrike is the most important character after the protagonist, it is not clear what gives him an origin. Because of his violence and shocking speeches, Shrike at times resembles Gurdjieff; he also seems to be a burlesque of A.R. Orage. Shrike is married, but he has a girlfriend, Miss Farkis, who resembles Orage's paramour and second wife, Jessie Dwight; Dwight worked in a book store and was Orage's secretary, and Shrike comments that Miss Farkis works in a book store. Miss Farkis also matches Jessie Dwight's physical description. Certainly Shrike discourses in a manner suggestive of an esoteric teacher, though his speeches are more like parodies than serious lectures.

We are confronted with Shrike from the very beginning, where he has placed a sadistic and mocking parody of a Catholic prayer on Miss Lonelyhearts's desk. Many of Shrike's most outrageous addresses are parodies of the Gurdjieff Work. The Work is called the Fourth Way and "the way of the sly man." (The word "sly" may have been be inserted in the text by West through the repeated use of such words as "furiously," "seriously," "enormously," "viciously," and "luxuriously"; this point is ambiguous.) The Fourth Way rejects the ways of the yogi, the monk, and the fakir. The Fourth Way develops the mind, body, and spirit at the same time. In *Miss Lonelyhearts* Shrike refers in a roundabout manner to The Fourth Way's dismissal of other methods:

> In this jungle, flitting from rock-gray lungs to golden intestines, from liver to lights and back to liver again, lives a bird called the soul. The Catholic hunts this bird with bread and wine, the Hebrew with a golden ruler, the Protestant on leaden feet with leaden words, the Buddhist with gestures, the Negro with blood. I spit on them all. Phooh! And I call upon you to spit. Phooh! Do you stuff birds? No, my dears, taxidermy is not religion. ("Miss Lonelyhearts and the Dead Pan")

But most striking is the way in which West's novel directly incorporates aspects of The Work for its own purposes. The novel is primarily driven by Gurdjieff's ideas about suffering. Suffering has a close relationship to what he called "sleep," the tendency for people to live like machines in a waking hypnotic sleep:

> Crowds of people moved through the street with a dream-like violence. As he looked at their broken hands and torn mouths he was overwhelmed by the desire to help them, and because this desire was sincere, he was happy despite the feeling of guilt which accompanied it. ("Miss Lonelyhearts Returns")

Again and again in discourses on The Work is the concept of men being machines met with but none more famously than in Ouspensky's *In Search of the Miraculous*:

> "A modern man lives in sleep, in sleep he is born and in sleep he dies. About sleep, its significance and its role in life, we will speak later. But at present just think of one thing, what knowledge can a sleeping man have? And if you think about it and at the same time remember that sleep is the chief feature of our being, it will at once become clear to you that if a man really wants

knowledge, he must first of all think about how to wake, that is, about how to change his being.

"Exteriorly man's being has many different sides: activity or passivity; truthfulness or a tendency to lie; sincerity or insincerity; courage, cowardice; selfcontrol, profligacy; irritability, egoism, readiness for self-sacrifice, pride, vanity, conceit, industry, laziness, morality, depravity; all these and much more besides make up the being of man.

"But all this is entirely mechanical in man. If he lies it means that he cannot help lying. If he tells the truth it means that he cannot help telling the truth, and so it is with everything. Everything happens, a man can do nothing either in himself or outside himself.["] (*In Search of the Miraculous* 73)

The above passage from Ouspensky includes many of the metaphors used throughout *Miss Lonelyhearts*: West emphasizes many times that his characters are machines—in particular he concentrates on Shrike's wife, Mary: "She was wearing a tight, shiny dress that was like glass-covered steel and there was something cleanly mechanical in her pantomime" ("Miss Lonelyhearts and Mrs. Shrike"). And West discusses machines throughout his narrative:

"Miss Lonelyhearts had again begun to smile. Like Shrike, the man they imitated, they were machines for making jokes. A button machine makes buttons, no matter what the power used, foot, steam or electricity. They, no matter what the motivating force, death, love or God, made jokes" ("Miss Lonely Hearts and the Clean Old Man"). However, the idea that the dream leads to violence is particularly striking, since it is difficult to see the connection. But the connection of violence to sleep is sharply made by Gurdjieff in Ouspensky's account:

"'What do you expect?" said G. "People are machines. Machines have to be blind and unconscious, they cannot be otherwise, and all their actions have to correspond to their nature. Everything happens. No one does anything. 'Progress' and 'civilization,' in the real meaning of these words, can appear only as the result of conscious efforts. They cannot appear as the result of unconscious mechanical actions. And what conscious effort can there be in machines? And if one machine is unconscious, then a hundred machines are unconscious, and so are a thousand machines, or a hundred thousand, or a million. *And the unconscious activity of a million machines must necessarily result in destruction and extermination.* It is precisely in unconscious involuntary manifestations that all evil lies. You do not yet understand and cannot imagine all the results of this evil. But the time will come when you will understand." (59; emphasis added)

Thus Miss Lonelyhearts wants to help relieve the suffering that he witnesses through the letters that he must answer, but he is powerless to act because —as stated above—"Everything happens, a man can do nothing either in himself or outside himself "(73). This Law of Accident is represented in the novel by Miss Lonelyhearts's childhood incident with a frog: "Miss Lonelyhearts felt as he had felt years before, when he had accidentally stepped on a small frog ("Miss Lonelyhearts and the Clean Old Man"). Unable to assist the frog, the boy obliterates it. But the issue here is that the event takes place because of an *accident.* Throughout the narrative, Miss Lonelyhearts is subject to the Law of Accident; he never rises above that law, and in the end he dies because he is subject to accident. This is a crucial theme in *Miss Lonelyhearts*— a theme that is not developed consistently in the novel, so that it may be overlooked. For instance, Miss Lonelyhearts asks a woman to sleep with him so that he will be "one gay dog." As we have seen, the dog theme is connected to the idea that without evolution one will die like a dog: the dog theme is thus intimately tied to the Law of Accident.

Finally, it remains to say something about the treatment of Gurdjieff in *Miss Lonelyhearts.* The name Gurdjieff was pronounced two different ways in English—gurd-jeef and gurdjeff: one of the odd things about the use of the phonetic *cabala* by the Oragean Modernists is that most of the writers indicated both pronunciations. Since the word "handkerchief" is the only English word that contains the phonemes "ker-chief," which closely approximates "gurd-jeef," nearly every Oragean Modernist text used the word "handkerchief" at some point to render Gurdjieff's name. West's *Miss Lonelyhearts* reverses many of the Oragean Modernist conventions: West allows the Clean Old Man to cough and to wipe his mouth on his black silk necktie. In other words, The Clean Old Man is denied the use of a *handkerchief*. The item is marked by its absence from the text. Similarly, The Clean Old Man is dragged out into the cold without an overcoat, a garment closely associated with Gurdjieff. During winters, overcoats were worn by Gurdjieff's followers indoors at the Prieuré (the chateau that housed the Institute for the Harmonious Development of Man outside of Paris). The overcoat symbolized the concept of the "false personality:" When the false personality was removed, it was said to be like taking off an overcoat. There are also phonetic clues in "The Clean Old Man" chapter that point to Gurdjieff: we are told that the old man poses like a "girl" (phonetically sounding Gur) and that he reacts at one point by "giggling (the initials G.I.G.), both common indications of Gurdjieff in other Oragean Modernist novels. Additionally, The Clean Old Man is given a cane, and this was characteristic of Gurdjieff, who is often shown with a cane, though Barnes perversely gives the cane to Orage's double in *Nightwood* (24). When asked his name, the old man replies that he is George Bramhall Simpson. "George" may be taken at face value. The name "Bramall" means "nook of land where broom grows," with the Old English noun *halh* meaning "secret place" (Mills *Place Names*). Thus his middle name gives some indication of the presence of the esoteric. "Simpson" is a rather complicated matter that is taken up at various points in the text itself: for instance, at one point we are told " If he could only believe in sin then everything could be simple and the letters extremely easy to answer" ("Miss Lonely Hearts on a Field Trip"). This obscure doctrine is derived from Gurdjieff's paradoxical idea about sin: "The chief difficulty for most people was the habit of talking. Voluntary silence can be the most severe discipline to which a man can subject himself. With everything there is a limit to what is necessary. After this, 'sin' begins. 'Sin' is something which is not necessary. People are afraid of suffering. They want pleasure not, at once and forever. They do not want to understand that pleasure is an attribute of paradise and that it must be earned" (Ouspensky ISM 356). As in many of the Oragean Modernist texts, Gurdjieff is ridiculed through his sexuality: Gurdjieff is handled roughly by Miss Lonelyhearts, who poses as a scientist and a psychologist and interrogates him about his putative homosexuality. This irreverent treatment of Gurdjieff through various sexual themes is one of the conventions of the Oragean Modernist novels that requires more study.

John O'Hara. *Appointment in Samarra* **(1934).** *"Appointment in Samarra* is a fast-paced, blackly comic depiction of the rapid decline and fall of Julian English. English is part of the social elite of his 1930s American hometown but from the moment he impetuously throws a cocktail in the face of one of his powerful business associates his life begins to spiral out of control— taking his loving but troubled marriage with it" (Vintage blurb). O'Hara's novel addresses Orage's Exercise 18, "The fact of death" and derives its mode of narration from reversing the technique of "self-observation and non-identification." It has been observed that O'Hara's novel provides a "somewhat enigmatic portrait" (Eppard 190). One factor contributing to English's enigmatic character is that the novel frames his actions such that all three of his crises (an assault, extra-marital sex, and suicide) are not shown and are only reported indirectly by other characters: thus the reader has no direct access to English at the most crucial points in the narration. This narrative device makes sense from the Gurdjieffian point of view but is inexplicable without any reference to esoteric theory. In other words, O'Hara is constructing his character in accordance with esoteric psychology, a subject which is unknown to the common reader.

O'Hara's black comedy is similar to that found in Nella Larsen's *Passing*, a novel that is often misread in such a way that its black comedy is overlooked. *Appointment in Samarra* is heavily coded with the phonetic *cabala*, and O'Hara uses the words "inexplicable" and "belching" to point to the use of the phonetic *cabala*. But O'Hara's novel has not much in the way of "legominism"—esoteric information. The novel uses the words "leg" and "miner" in close proximity to point to its minimal esoteric inclusions. O'Hara was more energetic in his employment of the phonetic *cabala*. The name of a young gangster is used to show that vowels do not matter: the man is called Al Grecco, but the name is meant to refer to the artist El Greco—so al and el are equivalent. At a slightly more difficult level of phonetic obscurity, Julian English is addressed as "Ju" few times in the novel, and English asks not to be called "Ju" presumably because it is phonetically equivalent to "Jew." People of his class are anti-Semitic, so it follows that English would not allow himself to be called a Jew. "Julian English" can be read through the phonetic *cabala* to say "Jew nail lash"—meaning "the Jews lashed Jesus and nailed him to the cross." O'Hara's phonetic *cabala* ties the characters to their names, so that when Julian English seeks out the man he assaulted so that he can apologize to him before the incident damages his business, he finds that Harry Reilly is rushing to catch a train and cannot speak to him: Harry Reilly, it follows, is in a "real hurry." Just as English hopes to speak to Reilly, Reilly comes out of his office and says, "Listen I can't wait another minute. I'm catching the ten-twenty-five and I have about four minutes" (171). In the case of another important name, O'Hara suggests that "Luther L. (L. for LeRoy) Fliegler..." (one of the salesmen at Julian English's Cadillac showroom with whom the novel opens and closes) serves as a bard or minstrel to the "court" of Julian English: at times in the text Fliegler is called "Lute" (a musical instrument associated with minstrels). And not only is his middle name a corrupted form of the French word for king, but when read as phonetic *cabala* his last name contains the word "liege"—a lord or sovereign to whom allegiance and service are due according to feudal law. Lute Fliegler's name appears at the opening of the novel to show the attentive reader the encoded phonetic *cabala* level of the text, and as Fliegler's point of view is an important component of the narration, his ironic name immediately establishes the novel's satiric handling of the small town society that Julian English rules over.

The section at the end of the novel where English realizes that he has not changed at all in his life is perhaps the section most in line with being an extended exposition of esoteric information, or a *legominism*: this passage is derived from the idea that "essence" and "personality" are opposed, and there can be no growth if, as in the case of Julian English, personality dominates essence:

> That was worse than anything he could do to Caroline, because it was something that did something to him. It made a change in himself, and we must not change ourselves much. We can stand only so many—so few changes. To know that there were people who he thought were his friends, his good friends, but who were his enemies—that was going to make a change, he knew. When was the last time there had been a change in himself. He thought and thought, rejecting items that were not change but only removal or adornment. He thought and thought, and the last time there had been a change in himself was when he discovered that he, Julian English, whom he had gone on thinking of as a child with a child's renewable integrity and curiosity and fears and all, suddenly had the power of his own passion; that he could control himself and use this control to give pleasure and a joyous hiatus of weakness to a woman. He could not remember which girl it had been; to forget her had been a simple manifestation of his ego; the important part of the discovery, the change, had been a thing for himself, his own moment. But he saw how deep and permanent the discovery, the change, became. It was almost as important, and no doubt precisely as permanent, as the simplest discovery of physical manhood. And there again it was the change and not the act that had been lasting and great; for he could not recall

with accuracy the circumstances of that discovery. (*Appointment* 220)

Even more telling is the statement in the following paragraph that "It was no *shock* to find out…" (220; emphasis added), since the shock is a crucial event and would have propelled English into the change that he so tragically lacked. The passage in Ouspensky that presents the relevant material on essence and personality is as follows:

> A very important moment in the work on oneself is when a man begins to distinguish his personality and his essence. A man's real I, his individuality, can grow only from his essence. It can be said that a man's individuality is his essence, grown up, mature. But in order to enable essence to grow up, it is first of all necessary to weaken the constant pressure of personality upon it, because the obstacles to the growth of essence are contained in personality. (Ouspensky 163)

Julian English having no "real I" in Gurdjieffian terms is *asleep*—and in the allegorical treatment of this theme it enough to bring him to suicide: in the case of normal people, according to Gurdjieff, they also are brought to suicide, but their suicide, being spiritual, is imperceptible to them and to others. Gurdjieff does not call this circumstance suicide; he says that it is "to die like a dog." In this way the novel doubles back on itself, for the third sentence of Chapter 1—by describing the wife as "working like a dog" (3) —puns on the Gurdjieff *work*, a doctrine that opposes "sleep" to "*work* on oneself":

> Our story opens in the mind of Luther L. (L for LeRoy) Fliegler, who is lying in his bed, not thinking of anything, but just aware of sounds, conscious of his own breathing, and sensitive to his own heartbeats. Lying beside him is his wife, lying on her right side and enjoying her sleep. *She has earned her sleep, for it is*

Christmas morning, strictly speaking, and all the day before she has worked like a dog, cleaning the turkey and baking things, and, until a few hours ago, trimming the tree. (Appointment 3; emphasis added)

In other words, Mrs. Fliegler has not worked like a dog, she has not *worked* at all (thus the trivialization of the tasks that she is credited with). She is asleep both literally and spiritually. Like Julian English she will die like a dog.

Dawn Powell. *Turn, Magic Wheel* . (1936). Dawn Powell seems to have inherited Carl Van Vechten's mantle as a satirist of the New York scene. Like Van Vechten she came from the Midwest, her first novels were about her home town, and her later novels were esoteric— from1936 on. Beginning to publish her novels in 1925, Powell was a prolific writer, and it would require an exhaustive study of her ten or so esoteric novels to determine how much of the inner workings of the Oragean Modernist movement she recorded in her novels. Here I will only report on two novels, *Turn, Magic Wheel*, New York: Farrar & Rinehart (1936) and *The Locusts Have No King*, New York: Charles Scribner's Sons (1948).

Turn, Magic Wheel is the story of an unsuccessful novelist, Dennis Orphen, who publishes a novel about his best friend, Mrs. Andrew Callingham / Miss Effie Thorne, the wife of a successful novelist. The title *Turn, Magic Wheel* is part of the refrain from a poem by Theocritus, "Idyl II, The Sorceress." Andrew Callingham, the absent husband, a figure based on Ernest Hemingway, is the lover to whom the novel's title and epigraph refer—"Turn, magic wheel, / Bring homeward him I love." When the wife finds that she has been exposed to ridicule by her companion, their relationship undergoes a serious strain. The novel is Gurdjieffian in its primary concern with observation: the protagonist-novelist is obsessed with peering into the lives of his acquaintances. It also reveals a concern with delusions. *Turn, Magic Wheel* maintains its distance from the Oragean Modernist circle and shows no direct interest in the esoteric. But this is immediately deceptive, for like all Oragean Modernist texts, the title announces the esoteric content. The interest in magic, which seems ancillary or contrived is underlined once the source is recognized. Where the wives of Andrew Callingham (the Hemingway surrogate) are powerless to deal with the egotistical novelist, the witch in Theocritus's poem uses her magical powers to force Delphis to return to her. But even more telling is the fact that in the poem the witch turns from her intial spell to another that adresses the Moon, and the poem replaces the original refrain with one that addresses the Moon, an address that continues for many lines—"*Bethink thee, mistress Moon, whence came my love.*" In the Gurdjieff-Orage system, the Moon is the central force in determining earthly affairs. It seems likely that Powell selected the title to allude to esoteric doctrines about the Moon. The title also invokes the Enneagram, the hieroglyphic wheel that was the most important of Gurdjieff's esoteric symbols. The association of the Enneagram with the wheel is a common device that is often met with in Oragean Modernist novels, as when Hurston elaborately presents chariot wheels in *Moses Man of the Mountain*.

Powell's novel uses the phonetic *cabala* to insert the names of Djuna Barnes, Elinor Wylie, Carl Van Vechten, and C. Daly King into the text, in addition to the contantly running presentations of Orage, Ouspensky ("nosebleed...pants" [135]), and Gurdjieff ("hakerchef" [sic] 135). The text also includes many phrases associated with the Gurdjieff Work, such as "secret knowledge," "seventh plane of being," "the sly man," "work," false personality ("second self" 129), "buffer" (130), and Ouspensky's book *In Search of the Miraculous: fragments of a lost knowledge* ("... secret fear of a pattern breaking up, fragments lost, plan forgotten." [133]). The most interesting effect in the novel takes place during a drunken discussion. The theme shifts to a consideration of the future, and Dennis Orphen opines that "It's the *snobhouse* for all of us...." (41; emphasis added). The word flophouse has mutated into snobhouse—a nonexistent word: this "lawful inexactitude" is used by Powell to refer to the Oragean idea that unless something is done to change the food that the Earth sends to the Moon everyone is doomed.

The name of the protagonist, Dennis Orphen, provides the key to the coded level of the novel: on page 18 we are offered "...not bad, the title page—by Dennis Orphen, author of *No Defense*." It is not readily apparent, since it has been universally missed by the readers of *Turn, Magic Wheel*, but Powell means for the reader to recognize that "Dennis Orphen" is equivalent to *No Defense*—that is why Orphen's first novel is being referred to. On page 64 Powell even uses the word "anagram," and this clue also does not serve to alert her readers to the esoteric level of the text, since stricly speaking the phonetic *cabala* is not composed of the strict rearrangements of the original letters in words that most people understand by the word "anagram." But if we can look past these reservations to try to take in Powells's style, the reader gets a real surprise. Dennis Orphen's first two sentences are esoteric fireworks: "Some fine day I'll have to pay, Dennis thought, you can't sacrifice everything in life to curiosity. For that was the demon behind his every deed, the reason for his kindness to beggars, organ-grinders, old ladies, and little children, his urgent need to know what they were knowing, see, hear, feel what they were sensing, for a brief moment to *be* them." Whether it is apparent or not, the two sentences allude to Gurdjieff (beggars— through his initials G.I.G.), to Orage (organ-grinders, urgent), to *Beelzebub's Tales to His Grandson: All And Everything: 1st Series* (everything, demon), to the "I am" exercise (to *be*), and to the "first exercise" that involves feeling, sensing, and counting pace ("see, hear, feel what they were sensing"). The entire novel is written by using this level of dense esoteric allusion, so that in effect, were one sensitive to the esoteric level, there would be nothing else in the text, for it rather obliterates the surface of the novel once it has been recognized: reading the novel in this way is reminiscent of Ludwig Wittgenstein's paradoxical and doubly-meaningful duck-rabbit.

Like Dennis Orphen (no defense), the other characters in *Turn, Magic Wheel* have names that are rendered as cliches when they are read using the phonetic *cabala*:

Mrs. Andrew Callingham ("call it a damned shame")

Tony Glaenzer ("not lazy")
Corrine Barrow ("narrow bore")
Asta Lundgren ("stand [your] ground")
Miss Effie Thorne ("run [like a] thief")
Olive Baker ("love [you] back")

Djuna Barnes. *Nightwood* **(1936).** *Nightwood* has a reputation for difficulty, as shown by this typical assessment:

> *Nightwood* is not truly a poem nor is it an Elizabethan or Jacobean tragedy, a satirical comedy, a Surrealist painting, or a circus performance. If the reader hopes to glean the rewards this mysterious gem of modernist literature surely contains, *Nightwood* must be approached with a more capacious and imaginative interpretive lens. We must wallow in the moments of total disorientation and relinquish all control to Barnes's acerbic wit and omnipresent irony in order to experience the text. We must resist the impulse to contain *Nightwood*'s strangeness within a succinct explanation, and instead embrace the feeling of total helplessness that comes with being at Barnes's authorial mercy. (Bellman "Spectacular Shadows.")

Djuna Barnes herself has proven to be as difficult to assess as her novel; her affiliations are but poorly understood. Some confusion about Barnes has been caused by the tendency to overlook Barnes in discussions of The Rope group, an esoteric group of lesbian writers and artists that worked closely with Gurdjieff in Paris. Fashions in literary study have focused two strains of inquiry on the personnel of The Rope group—*writing by women* and *modernist studies*. Rob Baker describes The Rope in these terms:

> During most of the Thirties and Forties in Paris, an extraordinary group of strong-willed women, mostly writers who also happened to be lesbians, became students of the spiritual teacher, G. I. Gurdjieff, meeting

privately with him as a small band that called themselves "The Rope." Their ties with Gurdjieff radically changed their lives, their writing styles, and their relationships to each other. (Baker "No Harem")

The membership of The Rope is said to have been Elizabeth Gordon, Solita Solano, Kathryn Hulme, Margaret Anderson, Georgette Leblanc, Louise Davidson and Alice Rohrer. Sometimes Jane Heap would come from London to attend meetings. The Rope's lesbianism has been seized upon, and there are lively studies of the group by literary scholars. And Rebecca Rauve points out that "Among them, the group's writers published 17 books after beginning to grapple seriously with Gurdjieff's teachings" (Rauve 46). Then, in the matter of modernist studies, the literary importance of The Rope is due to their connection to the international avant-garde:

> Jane Heap and Margaret Anderson, founding editors of the legendary *Little Review*, the literary journal which first published the poetry of Ezra Pound and T. S. Eliot in the United States, as well as the first chapters of James Joyce's *Ulysses* (the printing of which led to the editors' arrest and trial for alleged obscenity). The two had first met Gurdjieff in New York in 1924 and shortly relocated themselves and their magazine to Paris, partly to study with him at his institute at Fontainebleau, which he maintained until he was seriously injured in an automobile accident in 1929. (Baker "No Harem")

Insofar as Barnes's relationship to The Rope is concerned, the matter is treated vaguely when it comes up at all: Rauve states that

> The group, which began holding regular meetings in 1932, was designed as a sort of introduction to Gurdjieff's ideas and methods of self-study. Anderson and Leblanc were then living in Vernet, but the two attended meetings from time to time and later moved

back to the city to participate more fully. Webb suggests that Flanner and *Djuna Barnes may also have attended* (432), but their attitude toward Gurdjieff was skeptical, and if they did participate their presence was probably due more to respect for Heap's intelligence than to any interest in the teachings. ("Intersection"; emphasis added)

While Djuna Barnes lived in Paris and was associated with The Rope to an undetermined degree, her novel *Nightwood* bears all of the characteristics of the Oragean Modernist novel that I have outlined in Chapter One; while she may have been skeptical of Gurdjieff, as were all of the Orageans, her novel embodied Gurdjieff's teachings as they were disseminated by Orage. In reading *Nightwood* —particularly when doing close readings— critics have ignored the esoteric guideposts of the text and have thus been at a loss to say anything more than that *Nightwood* is chaotic and ironic. Looked at from the Oragean Modernist point of view, *Nightwood* is neither of these things; it is "objective," and it contains a good deal of the standard Gurdjieffian furniture, such as the "Parable of the Coach." Oragean Modernist writers often used Gurdjieff's parables as structural devices in their works. For instance, Hurston uses Gurdjieff's "the allegory of the house and its servants" in the "on the muck" section of *Their Eyes Were Watching God* and in the playhouse section of *Mules and Men*. Wallace Thurman also used the house allegory to structure *Infants of the Spring*, which took place in *Niggerati Manor* and was overseen by "The Pig Woman"— phonetic *cabala* for "I am G" (see Woodson *to Make a New Race* 67). Like Barnes, other Oragean Modernists based their works on the "Parable of the Coach." Rudolph Fisher's short story "Dust" replaces the coach with a motor car, and in Isa Glenn's novel, *East of Eden* a wealthy elderly woman heedlessly rides in a horse-drawn carriage through the congested New York avenues of the 1930s. Her coachman is named Higginson, a device which underlines the esoteric meaning of the coach, since all of the Oragean Modernist novels are replete with words containing "igg" (giggle, gig-mill, wiggle) as a way to write G. I. Gurdjieff through phonetic *cabala*. Barnes used the coach as the setting for an important episode in her novel, and given the anachronism that the coach presents, it is otherwise without explanation.

Nightwood has often been analyzed as a *roman a clef*, but since an esoteric context has never been applied, the results have been unsatisfactory: "At the very least, Djuna Barnes's *Nightwood* reveals the insufficiency of our cultural myths with which we might apprehend Barnes's art" (Bloomberg *Tracing*). Most of the difficulties of Barnes's texts are cleared up once it has been realized that the Count is G.I. Gurdjieff and that Dr. Matthew O'Connor is A.R. Orage. The first chapter of *Nightwood* reaches a climax when Count Onatorio Altamonte enters his home for the first time in the novel and ejects the guests that he was supposed to have been entertaining. Since the Count was not present, the guests have been listening to Dr. O'Connor tell an outlandish story. These events are Barnes's rendition of the most controversial event in the history of the Gurdjieff-Orage esoteric school, the New York meeting in 1931 at which Gurdjieff ejected the entire American membership of the Institute, because they were all supposedly being endangered by what they were studying under Orage. Here is an account of the event:

> Gurdjieff also engineered a situation which led to A.R. Orage's ultimate split from Gurdjieff in 1931. Gurdjieff visited Orage's groups in New York and perceived that the groups had become stuck and needed a shock to recover their spiritual momentum. He decided to ask the group members to sign a letter repudiating Orage as their leader. Ironically, Orage also signed the letter, sensing some hidden intent to Gurdjieff's actions. Eventually, Orage's relationship with Gurdjieff deteriorated and he saw Gurdjieff for the last time in May 1931. Despite a number of attempts by Gurdjieff to resume their relationship, they never spoke to each other again. In a conversation with fellow student C.S. Nott, Orage revealed his feelings about breaking with his teacher,

saying that "he felt that his work with groups in America had come to an end, and another phase was beginning; that to every pupil the time comes when he must leave his teacher and go into life and work out, digest, what he has acquired." (Staley "Negative Effects" 11)

Barnes adds a number of details that contribute to the identification of the Count and the doctor as Gurdjieff and Orage, respectively. The Count first slaps his *leg*, an indication of a "legominism," a feature of Gurdjieff's texts that here is used ironically to point to Gurdjieff himself (24). The Count then examines each of his guests with a magnifying glass; this is how Barnes describes the act of Gurdjieff ascertaining that Orage's students are "stuck." The Count retains one guest, a young woman in a riding habit. The doctor comments that as the Count fears that he is experiencing his last erection, he has kept the girl from leaving. The sexual aspect of this portrayal is in keeping with the original dispute that is believed by many at the time to have been that Gurdjieff and Orage were vying for the affections of a woman (Jessie Dwight), and that Orage ended up marrying her. This sordid episode is met with in a number of Oragean Modernists texts, and it is given considerable attention in West's *Miss Lonelyhearts*. As the episode was important to the case against Gurdjieff that Orage's followers built in their writings, in order to suggest the atmosphere surrounding this controversy, I will present the poem that Jessie Dwight wrote about Gurdjieff:

He call himself, deluded man,
The Tiger of The Turkestan.
And greater he than God or Devil
Eschewing good and preaching evil.
His followers whom he does glut on
Are for him naught but wool and mutton,
And still they come and sit agape
With Tiger's rage and Tiger's rape.
Why not, they say, The man's a god;
We have it on the sacred word.

His book will set the world on fire.
He says so - can God be a liar?
But what is woman, says Gurdjieff,
Just nothing but man's handkerchief.
I need a new one every day,
Let others for the washing pay.

(Dwight "Gurdjieff Poem")

The identification of the doctor as Orage is strengthened by the doctor's role in the novel: like Orage, Dr. O'Connor supplies a background of philosophical discourse that runs throughout the novel as a unifying motif; Orage appears in other Oragean Modernist novels discoursing in a similar manner, e.g., Glenn's *East of Eden*. To continue the *roman à clef* theme, we can identify Djuna Barnes as the character Nora Flood, whereas Nora's lover Robin Vote is a composite of Thelma Wood and the Baroness Elsa von Freytag-Loringhoven. But in keeping with the plan of the Oragean Modernist novel, Barnes has installed her characters in coded names:

Nora Flood (no love)
Robin Vote (rob love)
Jenny Petherbridge (ride any other)
Count Onatorio Altamonte (notorious cunt tamer)
Dr. Matthew Mighty-Grain-of-Salt-Dante-O'Connor (Don't you know at night all cats are gray.)

The Orage character, Dr. O'Connor, is seemingly treated with great disrespect in *Nightwood*: he spends a portion of the novel in bed dressed as a woman waiting for a sexual assignation. This treatment might be used to suggest that Barnes was as skeptical of Orage as she was of Gurdjieff. Running counter to this argument is the fact that the novel is a dense and intricate palimpsest of the teachings of the Oragean Hidden Learning—as C. Daly King liked to call it. The exacting inclusion of so much esoteric material in *Nightwood* argues positively for the idea that Djuna Barnes was an

Oragean. Her stylistic treatment of the esoteric materials remains a problem, but with the identification of the esoteric subtext of the novel it will be possible to resolve the many questions that remain.

Through the phonetic *cabala* the fabric of the *Nightwood* at every point enunciates the names of Orage, Ouspensky, Gurdjieff, and C. Daly King. The esoteric inclusions range from words inserted at the surface level to ideas presented piecemeal as phonetic *cabala*. The following list gives some idea of what has been included:

Cabala [cab-bulldog-hailed] (24); alchemy (83) [note that the word "alchemy" was not encoded], Fulcanelli [full-corn-heavily] (83); sleep (83, 34-5—and throughout the text), Chapter 2 "La Somnambule"); automism (64); octave— 1881 (1), [the novel consists of 8 chapters], 3 pianos [3x88] (5); interval (7); objective (7); remember himself (15); higher emotion (11); do something [According to Gurdjieff, "Man cannot do."] (18); what man really desires (19); magnetized (56); unobserved self (110); eternal recurrence (70); universal malady [This phrase is not given in its familiar form, but it refers to "chief feature," and to "kundabuffer": according to Gurdjieff there is an "universal malady" because man was wrongly made—hence the universal malady.] (32); book of magic (16); the dog [throughout the text—"Die like a dog." See below.].

The dog theme in *Nightwood* has befuddled many critics. The importance of the dog in the novel goes back to one of the most important themes in Gurdjieff and Orage's teachings:

> Gurdjieff taught that humans are not born with a soul, and are not really Conscious, but only *believe* they are Conscious because of the socialization process. Man must *create/develop* a soul through the course of his life by following a teaching which can lead to this aim, or he will "die like a dog". Gurdjieff taught that men are born *asleep*, live in *sleep* and die in *sleep*, only *imagining* that they are awake. He also taught that the ordinary waking "consciousness" of human beings was not consciousness

at all but merely a form of sleep and that actual higher Consciousness is possible. ("Fourth Way")

Interestingly, the doctor, the Orage-character, is associated with the cat—although this assignment is by no means obvious. The word "cat" is given in his extended name (*Dr. Matthew Mighty-Grain-of-Salt-Dante-O'Connor*) only through the "ct" in doctor—which is two degrees from visibility since "doctor" is rendered as "Dr." The translation of the name into the proverb is only possible through the inevitability of the phrase "at night all *cats* are gray"—because the phrase always implicates cats. There is no space to develop this discussion, but it is obvious that if the dog is death the cat might be expected to mean transcendence—though the only mention of the cat in the text is of "...Robin smiling sideways like a cat with canary feathers to account for..." (103). Even in this figure the cat is shown as being conscious, since it is being portrayed *through* its awareness (or consciousness) of the situation.

James Agee. *Let Us Now Praise Famous Men* [1936] (1941). Patrick Zimmerman comments that "In the 1960s, *Let Us Now Praise Famous Men* (with photography by Walker Evans), which had vanished without a trace when it first appeared in 1941, became enormously popular among a new generation of readers drawn to Agee's concern with spirituality and social justice" ("The Self-Dissatisfied Life and Art of James Agee"). Suzanne A. Austgen summarizes the background to the book:

> It was in 1936 that James Agee and Walker Evans, on assignment for *Fortune* magazine, drove into rural Alabama and entered the world of three families of white tenant farmers. And it was in this same year that Franklin D. Roosevelt was elected to his second term as president, his New Deal having won the resounding support of American voters. *Fortune* was not unique in its concern for the tenant farmer; Roosevelt himself appointed a Committee on Farm Tenancy to investigate the situation of this segment of the nation's farming population. The

committee's startling report, issued in February of 1937, revealed that tenant farmers constituted half of the farmers in the South, almost a third of farmers in the North, and a fourth of Western farmers. These figures, accompanied by reports of great suffering and stark poverty, led to the enactment of the Bankhead-Jones Farm Tenancy Act, which reorganized the Resettlement Administration as the Farm Security Administration, and which included among its purposes assisting enterprising tenants in becoming landowners. Agee and Evans examined the life of the tenant farmer as closely as the president's committee, but from the perspective of artists, not New Deal politicians or economists. Proposing no economic solutions to the problem of tenant farming, they attempted only to describe the life of the Gudgers, the Woods, and the Ricketts as accurately as possible "in its own terms." Nevertheless, the result of Agee and Evans' endeavors, a book entitled *Let Us Now Praise Famous Men*, is, as much as the New Deal itself, a great experiment in addressing the issues of social responsibility and human dignity that faced the United States during the 1930s. ("Agee and Evan's Great Experiment")

Let Us Now Praise Famous Men has been a difficult book to place in the literary canon due to its modernism as expressed through "experiment with new structural forms" and "deep self-consciousness" (Austgen). The elemental innovations of *Let Us Now Praise Famous Men* are routinely noticed and commented on, but the "spirituality" and "deep self-consciousness" of the text are floating signifiers without sufficient reference. Thus Matt Coogle concludes that "Agee and Evans reject any vision of the world as clearly understandable and ordered ("Historical Significance").

James Agee's biography betrays no direct connection to Orage's groups, in that his name appears in none of the extant lists. His associate, Walker Evans, was intimately connected with ballet director Lincoln Edward Kirstein, who had visited Gurdjieff in

Paris in the summer of 1927 and who attributed his work in dance to Gurdjieff: "Work done with George Balanchine since 1933 . . . was determined by what I gained from Gurdjieff's notions of conscious behaviour and physical possibility" (Kirstein). Anything more on this topic must be learned from examining *Let Us Now Praise Famous Men*.

Let Us Now Praise Famous Men was written to fulfill the Oragean Modernist plan for a literary text. That means in the first place that the text is written using the phonetic cabala. As clues to this condition, Agee has used the word "secret" twelve times and "decipher" (210) once. The specific indication of the phonetic cabala is an exaggerated use of "scab" six times on page 229 —"scab" being Agee's method of partially writing "cabala" in the phonetic cabala . "Scab" is to be combined with the other half of the word ("ala") from nearby elements. Running concurrently with the six uses of "scab" are the following words, in the order of their occurence: mules, mule, small, small, essential, mental, animal, literal, literal, literally, essential, malignant, malignant, all, identical, identical, all, all, wall, small. I have only resorted to two examples of the "ule" phoneme—there are many more; these would count the same as the "al" phoneme, but since most readers are not familiar with the rules of the phonetic cabala , I thought that it was more effective to only suggest their existence. I think that the extremity of Agee's performance in this instance demonstrates that he is willing to deform his text to any degree to accomplish his desired esoteric result.

Agee has altered the names of the three tenant farmer familes that appear in the text through the phonetic cabala. The three families are used to represent the followers of Gurdjieff, the followers of Orage, and those who are outside of the esoteric schools. Floyd Burroughs is called George Gudger. While "Gudger" is not literally (or letteraly) "Gurdjieff," it is closer than many other names used by Oragean Modernist writers to rename Gurdjieff; Walter Gilkyson calls him Giorgio Monte in the short story "Prisoner of Memory," and Nathaniel West calls him George Bramhall Simpson. The name "Ricketts" probably is meant to be read as "trick." There is an inescapable sense that information about Gurdjieff's school is being communicated through the names. Burt Westly Gudger seems the clearest message, and it revolves around the matter of "trust" —that is, the issue of whether or not Gurdjieff could be trusted: the name says "We trust Gurdjieff." The issue is particularly important in 1936, since Orage died in 1934, and apparently C. Daly King continued to have a following after 1934. Agee's book reflects his adherence to the Orage-King wing of the school, and thus it reflects King's antipathy towards Gurdjieff. King even believed that Gurdjieff suffered a frontal lobe injury from his 1924 accident that reduced his capacities and irrevocably changed him (Taylor *Gurdjieff's America* 68). The names in the Ricketts family contain a surplus of the syllable "ar" suggesting some connection to A.R. Orage. Apparently the Ricketts family has been set apart from the Gudger family, perhaps suggesting the split between the two camps of esotericists in America—the followers of Gurdjieff (the Gudgers) and the followers of Orage and King (the Ricketts). It is not immediately apparent how the Orageans have become identified as "tricksters," though perhaps it is simply the matter of their deceptive literary movement to which Agee refers.

The structure of the book is deceptive, for beneath the obvious divisions of the book that are shown in the table of contents, there is an esoteric structure—the succession of *legominisms* that construct the actual contents of *Let Us Now Praise Famous Men*. The *legominism* are indicated by approximations of the entire word *legominism*, as in the following example:

> ...*legs* were sharp with metal down. The blenched hair drew her face tight to her skull as a tied mask; her features were baltic. The young man's face was deeply shaded with soft short beard, and luminous with death. (33; emphasis added)

The material that follows the *legominism* marker concerns the esoteric idea of the three forces, as indicated in the text by "at the intersection of those three tones of force" (Agee 34). According to

Gurdjieff the two basic laws of reality are the law of three forces and the law of the octave: this passage alludes to the "law of three." Another *legominism* marker reverses the order of the syllables:

> …and the body of Emma, her sister, strong, thick and wide, tall, the breasts set wide and high, shallow and round, not yet those of a full *woman*, the *legs* long thick and strong; and Louise's green lovely body, the dim breasts faintly blown between wide shoulders, the thighs long, clean and light in their line from hip to knee, (Agee 57; emphasis added)

The material that follows is related to the esoteric idea of "sleep."

Let Us Now Praise Famous Men is above all a record of an exercise in "self-observation" carried out by James Agee and Walker Evans. Knowing this and saying this does not in essence bring us to a solution of the problems set forth by the text. This is because "self-observation" is itself a controversial in the practice of spiritual development: there are endless discussion of what it is, where it originated, how it is practiced, its relationship to "self-remebering," and its relationship to psychology and spirituality. This is not the place to resolve anything of such complexity. I can only point out that Agee's text not only enacts the course of self-observations that he carried out in 1936, it also serves as a repository for esoteric materials. These functions are in every way misaligned, so that like the novels that were the more usual productions of the Oragean Modernist writers, the contradictory narratives that were poured into the textual containers were never effectively resolved for any of the separate functions. The novels were seldom satisfactory novels, and though we can never know how well they served as esoteric repositories, the suspicion is that they were not very useful as such. Similarly, no useful judgments can be made about the effectiveness of *Let Us Now Praise Famous Men* as an esoteric document. And in order to make any assessment of it as a modernist literary work, it would be necessary to completely re-theorize Modernism: of course, the Oragean

Modernists have already re-theorized Modernism in terms of "Objective art," but their theorization only serves the purposes of esotericists. As outsiders who do not even have access to the complete esoteric discourse, literary critics and scholars are not in a position to seriously take on the task of hermetic re-theorization. Given the drive of literary scholars to produce "definitive" studies of literary texts, it gives one pause to contemplate the scholarly establishment faced with a body of writing with which they are always already faced with hermeneutic failure.

I will thus conclude my comments on *Let Us Now Praise Famous Men* by making some general observations about the text. It seems to me that Agee's book may best be approached if there is some appreciation for the exercise known as "self-observation without identification." Orage defined self-observation as follows:

> The aim of self-observation, however, apart from its results, is clear; to see ourselves as others. When I can be, for myself, my neighbor, and my neighbor, for me, myself, I shall have attained the objectivity of a normal human being. Thereafter the development of the spirit and soul will be as normal as is now the growth and development of the body. (Driscoll "Aphorisms")

Thus we can see that again and again in his text Agee struggles to place himself in the position of the other. The whole meaning of *Let Us Now Praise Famous Men* comes into focus if the reader has some notion of the exercises that serve as the background for Agee's practice. The following are some notes taken by a student of Orage's in the course of lectures given in new York in 1927 as relating to the method for carrying out self-observation:

> Taking up the six observations again. Gestures often offset speech, give wrong impressions of what you say. We give ourselves away with our hands while saying something different. Gestures responsible for wrong impressions conveyed. Examination of gestures necessary for intelligent life. Watch yourself, and make

list of all your various gestures for one week. Then you will have a complete vocabulary of your gestures. Note similar gestures in someone else and know what they mean.

Regarding postures: Every race has specific postures. We don't sit like Indians. We sit like Americans. See man standing before a fire. You can tell at once whether he is American or English. Note a man sitting. Can tell where educated, even from what college attended. Characteristic postures change with emotions. The more one leans back in a chair, the more the person seems at home. Posture precedes impression one wishes to make.

Regarding voice: One may have wonderful vocabulary, but tone of voice would queer it. One would believe opposite of what said if said in certain tone of voice. One would say, "He did not mean that." Sincere tones are believed. Know your sincere tones and be able to convey what you mean, your object.

Facial expressions are an elaborate language. "Did you see how he looked?" A single facial expression can be considered a gesture. A wink might mean, "meet you outside," etc. Make serious effort to write down tones of voice, gestures, postures, facial expressions, this week and get complete vocabulary. (The other two, movements and sensations, were not mentioned.)

Need not write observations down at the time, later from memory will do. Lie in wait for opportunity to note voice, postures, gestures, facial expressions, under extreme conditions. Record moments of jealousy, anger, surprise, disappointment, etc. (Schneider "Passion")

This list compares favorably with what is found in Agee's text. When Agee encounters a young black couple while he is walking down the road, his description of them is in line with the ideas presented above. He can be seen methodically applying the "six observations" to a moment of *surprise* —as Orage has suggested:

> They just kept looking at me. There was no more for them to say than for me. The least I could have done was to throw myself flat on my face and embrace and kiss their feet. That impulse took hold of me so powerfully, from my whole body, not by thought, that I caught myself from doing it exactly and as scarcely as you snatch yourself from jumping from a sheer height: here, with the realization that it would have frightened them still worse (to say nothing of me) and would have been still less explicable; so that I stood and looked into their eyes and loved them, and wished to God I was dead. After a little the man got back his voice, his eyes grew a little easier, and he said without conviction that that was all right and that I hadn't scared her. She shook her head slowly, her eyes on me; she did not yet trust her voice. Their faces were secret, soft, utterly without trust of me, and utterly without understanding; and they had to stand here now and hear what I was saying, because in that country no negro safely walks away from a white man, or even appears not to listen while he is talking, and because I could not walk away abruptly, and relieve them of me, without still worse a crime against nature than the one I had committed, and the second I was committing by staying, and holding them. (Agee 42)

For convenience, *Let Us Now Praise Famous Men* may be thought of as three texts running concurrently—the phonetic *cabala* of the names of esoteric teachers, Agee's course of self-observations, and esoteric ideas presented in various ways. In some instances esoteric ideas are inserted into the text as figures of speech, as when "magnetic obligation" (27) is used in an offhand manner. The text includes many useages of estoeric ideas such as "shock "(37), "magnetic center" (53), "work" (34), "attention" (35), "effort" (219), "food" (294), "imprisonment" (294), "moon" (294), and work "'for yourself'" (292). Agee, of course, wrote his text as though it is not an esoteric text, so the esoteric vocablary is not generally noticed by the reader for what it is: but Agee has taken care to indicate to the reader that *Let Us Now Praise Famous Men* is an esoteric text, and to that point he states that "tenant" is "one of the words a careful man will be watchful of" (415)—the idea being that the "careful man" alone will be able to penetrate to the esoteric levels of the book. Having said this he then sets up a tremendous list of words that need to be watched closely (415-17).

The Yearling. **Marjorie Kinnan Rawlings (1938).** *The Yearling* is distinguishable from other works of Oragean Modernism by its continuing popularity. Christopher B. Rieger states that

> Rawlings always maintained that *The Yearling* was not only a book for boys, but, first and foremost, a novel that happened to have a young boy as the main character. Despite her protests, the book has become nearly exclusively identified with juvenile or adolescent fiction. Its coming-of-age theme, sometimes obvious symbolism, and occasionally hackneyed writing (e.g., "The words were as strengthening as the sweet potato. 'I'm all right now, Pa.'"), however, rank the novel a notch below two other notable examples of works that have been co-opted into the category of adolescent fiction, *Gulliver's Travels* and *The Adventures of Huckleberry Finn*. This is not to suggest that *The Yearling* is "merely" a children's book, for it is certainly much more than that, both in Rawlings' intention and her execution. (117)

Rawlings's conception was to write an esoteric novel that developed the theme of "essence and personality." The novel's treatment of this theme is complicated by its parallel need to address the cosmic setting of human life. Rieger points out the relationship between the themes of adulthood and awareness of the cosmos:

> Jody's final adventure of the novel occurs on the river as he determines to flee his home after he kills Flag. He plans to flee to Boston to pursue a romanticized vision of life at sea with the friend he idolizes, Oliver Hutto. Unlike the river scenes in *South Moon Under* and *Cross Creek* , the water does not provide solace or liberation, but it is still a place where the certainty of fixed categories disintegrates. In the aftermath of Flag's death, Jody sees only that his father has betrayed him, undermining the sense of safety and order Jody associates with home: "Without Penny, there was no comfort anywhere. The solid earth had dissolved under him" (415). As Jody paddles a small canoe towards the middle of Lake George in search of a passenger ship that will pick him up, the vast expanse of water symbolizes the terrifying and solitary world of adulthood: "He was out in the world, and it seemed to him that he was alien here, and alone, and that he was being carried away into a void… [T]he open water seemed to stretch without an end" (416-7). Jody's panic increases as the waves intensify and his canoe starts taking on water, and he madly paddles back to the relative comfort of the shoreline. (122-23)

One element of *The Yearling* that demonstrates the esoteric thrust of the text are the intricate and expressive names that Rawlings gave to her characters. The title of the novel itself is phonetic *cabala* for "Earthling." Given the interest that Gurdjieff had in space travel and in narrating his book *Beelzebub's Tales* from the perspective of a character located on Mars, it is logical that such an "objective" perspective had been adopted by Rawlings for a novel about the human situation. The names that Rawlings used to reveal her esoteric view of reality are as follows:

Penny Baxter (pay back). Penny Baxter embodies the Gurdjieffian understanding of man's place in the cosmos:

> Gurdjieff said that one should look at the world in the same way that one would look at another person or at oneself. The world was, in a sense, only a reflection or an enlargement of the individual world in each of us. Just as there were two sides to a person, there were two sides to the earth. To bring each of these sides together so that they might live in peace and harmony was the one fundamental purpose of all messiahs and messengers from the gods. He said that the time was very short. That it was necessary to achieve this world harmony as soon as possible to avoid a complete disaster. (Patterson "The Last Esoteric Message")

Ora Baxter (terror). Another major theme in the Gurdjieff work is the so-called "terror of the situation." Ora looks right at this situation, while Flag prevents Jody from being able to see it; at the same time Flag embodies the "terror of the situation"—and his death by shocking Jody into wakefulness manifests the "terror of the situation" for Jody.

> *The terror of the situation*, in Gurdjieff's phrase, is that we're consigned to a world run, for the most part, by sleeping people; people who are never awake at all. They walk, they talk, they make "decisions"–they react, mechanically, to stimuli. They are driven by odd little constructions formed around vanity and fear. They're often nearly psychotic–yet they can rise to positions of great power and influence. (Perhaps the media fascination with zombies is some unconscious apprehension of the danger represented by mindless, sleepwalking humanity.) All of us are subject to a tendency to slip into a comforting trance, the walking sleep of daily life. (Shirley "What If It's True?")

Jody Baxter (tax body—the implication is that the body should make "super-efforts" as Jody does when he runs away from home and travels a great distance without food.)

Flag (gulf—appearing in the text as the "void")

Lem Forrester (moral fester)

Buck Forrester (bicker)

Grandma Hutto (G [Gurdjieff] ran out)

Oliver Hutto (love/hate)

Old Slewfoot (fools well)

Fodder-wing (The name of this character requires more discussion. In the text he is described in terms of his disabilities:

> "The youngest Forrester had conceived the idea that if he could attach himself to something light and airy, he could float from the roof-tree of the barn as gently as any bird. He had attached great bundles of fodder, cow-pea hay, to his arms, and jumped. He had survived, miraculously, adding a few broken bones further to contort the hunch-backed frame with which he had been born. It was a crazy thing to do, of course. Yet privately, Jody felt, something of the sort might work. He had, himself, often thought of kites, very large kites. And some secret understanding was his of the crippled boy's longing for flight; for lightness; for a moment's freedom from his body, earth-bound and bent and stumbling." (*The Yearling* Chapter 5)

The idea of finding release through food is the principle behind the alchemy that underlies the Gurdjieff Work. Here is a summary of the esoteric idea of "food":

> But whereas the descent of humanity takes place *en masse*, ascent or evolution is possible only within the individual. *In Search of the Miraculous* presents a series of diagrams dealing with the same energies and laws as the Ray of Creation, not only as a cosmic ladder of descent but also in their evolutionary aspect *within the*

individual. In these diagrams, known collectively as the Food Diagram, Ouspensky explains in some detail how Gurdjieff regarded the energy transactions within the individual human organism. As in the Ray of Creation, the Food Diagram arranges the data of modern science, in this case the science of physiology, in a manner that subsumes these data naturally within the immensely vast scale of ancient metaphysical and cosmological principles. Again, the reader is referred to Ouspensky's book, the point being that humanity can begin to occupy its proper place within the chain of being only through an inner work with the specific intrapsychic energies that correspond to the higher energies in the cosmic order and which within the individual human being may be subsumed under the general term *attention.* The many levels of attention possible for man, up to and including an attention that in traditional teachings has been termed Spirit, are here ranged along a dynamic, vertical continuum that reaches from the level of biological sustenance which humans require for their physical bodies up to the incomparably finer sustenance that they require for the inner growth of the soul. This finer substance is termed "the food of impressions," a deceptively matter-of-fact phrase that eventually defines man's unique cosmic obligation and potentiality of constantly and in everything working for the development within himself of the divine attributes of devotion to the Good and objective understanding of the Real. (Needleman "School")

What Fodder-wing was reaching for by fastening himself to cow-pea hay is the "incomparably finer sustenance" of "the energy transactions in a moment of authentic consciousness" (Needleman "School"). Read exoterically, the novel presents Fodder-wing as physically and mentally disabled. The esoteric meaning behind this portrayal is perhaps too obscure to be worked out without full knowledge of the Gurdjieff Work: as stated above, man as he exists in nature is not from the "objective" point of view a "normal man." Only the man developed in an esoteric school can have evolved into a "normal human being." Fodder-wing symbolizes the state of man as he is found in nature—severely disabled. And Fodder-wing aspires to attain the state of the "normal human being," which is how he comes to the absurd act of attaching himself to a "finer sustenance" in the form of cow-pea hay, the hay being also a symbol. Fodder-wing is surrounded by psychopaths who see themselves as being normal, so his utterances and strivings appear to be insane. He seems to be striving after something impossible for him as an individual—physical, mental, and emotional wholeness, —when it is the general condition of humanity to be "disabled" like Fodder-wing from the "objective" perspective.

The theme of "essence" that is the central concern of *The Yearling* is a vast topic. Briefly, Gurdjieff states that "Fate is the result of planetary influences which correspond to a man's type. Fate only relates to a man's essence. A man consists of two parts: essence and personality. Essence in a man is what is his own. Personality in man is what has come from the outside, what he has learned or reflects. Essence is the truth in man" (Ouspensky 161). The theme of "essence" has interested other Oragean Modernists, and in *Firecrackers* Van Vechten has created a prodigy, Consuelo, to represent this theme. Consuelo (soul) is destroyed by her parents since she is not allowed the proper growth of her essence; her superior intelligence and intuition have been allowed to overshadow her innate qualities. Another treatment of this theme is Bernice Lesbia Kenyon's short story, "The Doll." It would seem that Rawlings had been assigned a full-length treatment of the theme of "essence." The novel requires a close study with this topic as the focus.

Ralph Ellison. *Invisible Man* **(1952).** It is said from time to time that *Invisible Man* is a *roman a clef*, yet most commentators identify only one character as a real person, and in *Wrestling with the Left* Barbara Foley identifies two. The illogic of this treatment speaks to the problems that have incurred because of the concern with Marxism with which critics have addressed themselves to this prizewinning canonical text. *Invisible Man* is a complex *roman a clef*, and the novel's many characters may be identified as the members of an esoteric group with a specific ideology. This reassignment of the "conditional fictionality" (Genette 24) of the text as a *roman a clef*—"a true story for some and a fiction for others" (Genette 24)—fundamentally revises our understanding of Ellison's text, particularly since there is even a view that the text does not need to be thought of or evaluated as a *roman a clef*:

> *Invisible Man* is badly served by any attempt to turn it into a *roman clef*. The invisible man lives on because he is Candide, Everyman, and many young black Communists (including Dick Wright), and may speak for all of us on the lower frequencies. Yet we underestimate Ellison's craft if we fail to realize how many striking images generally assumed to derive exclusively from *belles lettres* or folklore also had a political life in the Red 1930s and post-Red 1940s: the kill-the-bearer letters, the bogey man in the electrified coal hole, black leaders in eclipse, moonstruck dreams courtesy of a white banker, and the confused poster boys of the Marxist cult of martyrdom, a.k.a. "Tod Clifton," a.k.a. "Gene Braxton," to whom I must return. (Griffiths "Ralph Ellison")

In other words, if the text was written precisely to present certain individuals lightly disguised as characters, then the treatment of the text since its publication has been misguided at best.

Ellison's novel is episodic, and in general each episode revolves around the protagonist's confrontation with one important character. The novel is composed of twenty-five chapters, a prologue, and an epilogue. While *Invisible Man* is appreciated for its modernist stylistic innovations, from the esoteric point of view it conforms to the Oragean Modernist plan. *Invisible Man* is written in the phonetic *cabala*, and instructions for reading the phonetic *cabala* are given in the "cabin" passage on 35 and the "cab" passage on 518, the key in both descriptions being "sound."

The novel contains *legominisms* marked by some rendering of the word "legominism—usually "leg" or "lecture." *Invisible Man* contains a running presentation of the names of esoteric teachers in the phonetic *cabala*. And it recapitulates the ideas of the Gurdjieff Work.

Invisible Man differs from other Oragean Modernist novels in that the Fourth Way ideas are more integral components of the narrative. For instance, the idea of the "shock" is wedded to the action of the "Battle Royal" chapter, Chapter 1. Conventional readings of that chapter focus on the symbolism of the artifacts that the protagonist encounters—the blindfold, the white woman, the free-for-all, and the speech. But from the esoteric point of view these sociological considerations are overshadowed by the "shock" that is delivered to the protagonist by the episode. The literal electric shock received when the boxers try to recover the money thrown into the ring serves to anchor the allegorical presentation of the esoteric idea of the "shock":

> Gurdjieff maintains that as the energy and matter of the universe transform up and down the cosmic scale, it requires an extra push or *shock* when it reaches the shortened intervals in order to continue its transformation. The requirements of these *shocks* are of critical importance in relation to the higher evolution of humans beings. (MacFarlane. "Gurdjieff's Cosmology"; emphases added)

There is a similar narrative treatment of other Fourth Way ideas in the novel, such as the idea that man is a "machine" in the paint factory episode, and the idea of "food" in the rooming-house episode.

By far the most unusual and interesting innovation in *Invisible Man*'s fulfillment of the plan of the esoteric realist novel is Ellison's handling of the followers of A.R. Orage through the narrative device of the *roman a clef*. Ellison's use of disguises is complex, so complex in fact that he announces his intentions as he performs them—though perhaps it is not clear what he is saying when he does this. When the protagonist is escaping from the police after giving his rabble-rousing speech in Chapter 13, he is confronted with arguably the most important character in the narrative, Brother Jack. Before he actually meets Brother Jack, but realizes that a stranger is following him over the roofs, he observes that "If only it were like at home where I knew someone in *all* the houses, knew them by sight and by name, by blood and by background, by shame and pride, and by religion" (279). Interpreted esoterically this sentence is Ellison's announcement that the members of the Oragean school are present in the novel and are identified "by sight and by name." Ellison presents the names of the members of Orage's school fairly clearly, though at times he obscures their appearances so that they strain easy recognition. The identities of Ellison's characters are as follows:

G.I. Gurdjieff. Ellison begins his introduction of Gurdjieff as Brother Jack by having Brother Jack offer the protagonist his name —as food:

> I watched him going across the floor with a bouncy, rolling step then found a table and sat watching him. It was warm in the cafeteria. It was late afternoon now and only a few customers were scattered at the tables. I watched the men going familiarly to the food counter and ordering. His movements, as he peered through the brightly lighted shelves of pastry, were those of a lively small animal a fyce, interested in detecting only the target cut of cake. So he's heard my speech; well, I'll hear what he has to say, I thought seeing him start toward me with his rapid, rolling, bouncy, heel-and-toey step. It was as though he had taught himself to walk that way and I had a feeling that somehow he was acting a part; that something about him wasn't exactly real—an idea which I dismissed immediately, since there was a quality of unreality over the whole afternoon. He came straight to the table without having to look about for me, as though he had expected me to take that particular table and no other—although many tables were vacant. He

was balancing a plate of cake on top of each cup, setting them down deftly and shoving one toward me as he took his chair.

"I thought you might like a piece of cheese cake," he said.

"Cheese cake?" I said. "I've never heard of it."

"It's nice. Sugar?"

(282)

Ellison has made a point of describing Gurdjieff as a dog—a fyce, a type of small hunting dog—, though this point will elude the exoteric reader: in esoteric terms this appellation is highly derogatory. The name "Gurdjieff" is rendered by Brother Jack as "gar-cheese"—From "cheese cake" and "sugar." Here Ellison uses the pronunciation that is approached by the last two syllables of "handkerchief" —the pronunciation of "Gurdjieff" that is considered more authentic. The physical description of Brother Jack is misleading, since his salient attribute is his red hair. Assuming a Communist political context for the novel as do most critics, Frederick Griffiths states that "The reference to Herndon and Lenin is not fortuitous, for the invisible man starts running in Angelo's direction politically once he gets "discovered" by the redhaired/Red Brother Jack." But in the esoteric context Gurdjieff is red because he is the author of *Beelzebub's Tales*, and in religious symbology Satan has a red head. What Ellison says about Brother Jack is an echo of the many accounts of Gurdjieff's students setting down their first encounters, but it most resembles Ouspensky's:

I remember this meeting very well. We arrived at a small cafe in a noisy though not central street. I saw a man of an oriental type, no longer young, with a black mustache and piercing eyes, who astonished me first of all because he seemed to be disguised and completely out of keeping with the place and its atmosphere. I was still full of impressions of the East. And this man with the face of an Indian raja or an Arab sheik whom I at once seemed to see in a white burnoose or a gilded turban, seated here in this little cafe, where small dealers and commission agents met together, in a black overcoat with a velvet collar and a black bowler hat, produced the strange, unexpected, and almost alarming impression of a man poorly disguised, the sight of whom embarrasses you because you see he is not what he pretends to be and yet you have to speak and behave as though you did not see it. He spoke Russian incorrectly with a strong Caucasian accent; and this accent, with which we are accustomed to associate anything apart from philosophical ideas, strengthened still further the strangeness and the unexpectedness of this impression. (7)

When Gurdjieff was in New York, he often set himself up in cafeterias to meet with people, just as he does with the protagonist. Other aspects of the meeting that follow the passage quoted above include elements familiar in accounts of Gurdjieff. *Invisible Man* has a far more complex narrative structure than has been observed; in the subplot that is directed toward the Oragean's intervention in "objective history" the Brother Jack character takes on multiple roles. It may be noticed that when first introduced, Sybil tells the protagonist that her husband is "Hubert" (401). Later she calls him George (513), and the protagonist takes no notice of this new name. We may also note that when the protagonist is in bed with Sybil and her husband looks into the room, the protagonist is unable to grasp the nature of the man or of the events unfolding. But the explanation is that Brother Jack is also the husband Hubert-George. He is called Hubert as a clue to his "objective" role in the historical drama as the *Herod* character to his wife, Sybil's role as Salome—a matter that will be explicated in the following chapter. And his "George" name reveals that he is also George Ivanovich Gurdjieff.

Carl Van Vechten (176-191). It is curious that there has not been much critical interest in Mr. Emerson's son; this is perhaps because the "unspeakable" (184) nature of the character introduces themes that critics do not wish to engage. Lists of the characters in

Invisible Man never take note of him. The physical description of Mr. Emerson's son—"the blond man" (178) with an effeminate walk (177)—accurately fits Van Vechten. Van Vechten's name does not seem to be offered in a cipher; it is the Calamus club, with its unmistakable insinuation of homosexuality that is the chief clue to the identity of Emerson's son.

A.R. Orage (368-68). In *Invisible Man* it is Ras the Exhorter who represents A.R. Orage. Ellison's handling of the Gurdjieff-Orage split is obscured by his use of race to represent esotericism. But the identification is made plain when the black nationalist, Ras the Exhorter, addresses himself to the protagonist and Tod Clifton: "I ask both of you, are you awake or sleeping?" (366). Orage actually published a short piece called "Are We Awake" (1925) in which he asks, "How can we prove to ourselves at any given moment that we are not asleep and dreaming? Life circumstances are sometimes as fantastic as dream circumstances; and change with the same rapidity. What if we should wake up and find waking life a dream, and our present sleep and dream merely dreams within a dream?" (Orage). Ras the Exhorter is phonetic *cabala* for "A.R. Orage."

C. Daly King (344-48). Arriving in New York in 1936, Ralph Ellison would not have studied with A.R. Orage who left New York in 1931 and died in 1934. The narrative of *Invisible Man* suggests that Ellison studied with C. Daly King. In the text it is Brother Hambro who is used to present King, and Ellison has selected the word "working" (348) as the particularly apt device to suggest both the Gurdjieff *Work* and C. Daly *King* in one word. Ellison describes Hambro as "the Brotherhood's chief theoretician" (348), a role that also applies to King who was responsible for recording and disseminating Orage's lectures as the unpublished volume, *The Oragean Version*.

Muriel Draper. Muriel Draper was an important organizer of the New York school and for many years a *saloniste*. She appears in many of the Oragean Modernist novels in her role as a *saloniste*, and in Van Vechten's *Firecrackers* as an organizer of an esoteric school. Ellison has radically altered the circumstances with which Muriel Draper surrounded herself, for her salon was famous for its shabby condition. In *Invisible Man*, Emma, the Muriel Draper character is wealthy and her apartment is palatial. Her identity is given when the protagonist notices "…Italian-red *draperies* that fell in rich folds from the ceiling" (294; emphasis added). The meeting between the protagonist and Emma is announced as a *legominism* since Ellison writes, "Somewhere in my *leg* a muscle twitched violently" (295; emphasis added). The *legominism* apples to the protagonist's comment on the fact that Emma looks at him in the manner that was characteristic to the way that Gurdjieff was reputed to be able to size up people: "it was something more, a direct what-type-of-mere-man-have-we-here kind of look that seemed to go beneath my skin . . ." (295). The notion of appearances and reality in personalities was always made an issue in the Gurdjieff Work, as this quote from H.L. Finch amplifies:

> Gurdjieff himself wore a very evident 'disguise' which, as it seems, automatically excluded those people who could not see through it. It was just the disguise of the 'charlatan' which kept the largest numbers away . . . Such a faint aura of distrust (around the one man in all the world who could perhaps, when it came down to it, be most surely trusted!) served its purpose. Only the real searchers could see through it. (23)

Zora Neal Hurston. Hurston is enacted by the character Mary Rambo. "Hurston" is given through phonetic *cabala* when the phrase "hard times" is spoken three times by Mary Rambo (252). The name "Mary" points to the Virgin Mary, and "Rambo" is phonetic *cabala* for "womb." These assignments come into focus once Hurston is paired with the unpublished novel about the life of Herod Antipas on which she worked from 1955 until her death in 1965. Hurston scholars have speculated in vain as to the nature of Hurston's motive for undertaking such a seemingly eccentric project. But Hurston's project follows from her major role in the Oragean Modernist movement and from the centrality of Herod in the "objective historical drama" that the Orageans Modernists were arranging.

Melvin B. Tolson. Tolson is not especially recognizable as "the vet," the mental patient that the protagonist meets at the Golden Day. Because "the vet" was a doctor, the protagonist solicits his help in dealing with the stricken Mr. Norton. The identification of "the vet" as Tolson is made when "the vet" answers a question with the one-word answer, "Nostalgia" (90)—which is phonetic *cabala* for 'Tolson." Much of what "the vet" says are ideas from the Gurdjieff Work thinly disguised as Freudian psychoanalytic theory; the vet speaks of "shocks," man as a machine ("the boy, this automaton" [93]), and the awareness of the descent into chaos—Gurdjieff's "the terror of the situation."

George Schuyler. Harlem Renaissance novelist George Schuyler is Peter Wheatstraw. Chapter Nine begins with a description of the setting that contains "sky," "skyscrapers," "school," "clear," "clear," "girls," "early," and "workaday." These are all clues—some running in reverse—that deliver the name, "Schuyler." Ellison even alludes to his use of the phonetic *cabala* in the passage, when he mentions the bellow of a bull "*sounding* clear and full above bells" (169; emphasis added), the idea being that the sounds of the phonemes in the phonetic *cabala* must be allowed to ride above the other elements of a passage: note that Ellison uses "bull" and "bells" to demonstrate that in phonetic *cabala* the words are equivalent. Peter Wheatstraw has a cart filled with plans, yet he denigrates the plans and the whole idea of planning. Later he gives himself away as a conjurer. Even though he seems to advise the protagonist that plans *must* be changed, the overriding sense of the episode is that Peter Wheatstraw has an "objective" role in history and an "objective" understanding of events. The cart filled with plans that are being thrown away echoes of a passage in *Turn, Magic Wheel* , where Dawn Powell takes the opposite view toward plans: "…secret fear of a pattern breaking up, fragments lost, plan forgotten" (133). Powell alludes to Ouspensky's book *In Search off the Miraculous: fragments of a lost knowledge* and she also touches on the esoteric idea that it is "those who know" who sustain the Earth. Thus the implication here is that the plans are really esoteric knowledge, and it is the contents of the cart that must be protected and never disposed of.

In confirmation of the initiatory importance of the plans, as he departs Peter Wheatstraw sings a song that repeats "Legs/ legs, legs...," a sure sign that his character and his speeches contain a *legominism*. He is the apostle Simon Peter in the Oragean Modernist's "objective" drama. The name "Wheatstraw" follows from Schuyler's association with Simon Peter, for "In the Gospel of Luke 22:31, Jesus's prediction of Peter's denial is coupled with a prediction that all the apostles ("you", plural) would be "sifted like wheat," but that it would be Peter's task ("you", singular), when he had turned again, to strengthen his brethren."

Angelo Herndon. The paragraph that sets up the late arrival of Tod Clifton on page 353 gives the name "Angelo Herndon" in exceptionally diffuse phonetic *cabala*: **An** (spokesman, begin, present, unit), **g** (Gothic), **el** (well well, still, he'll, shall, small, ceiling, hall), **o** (folding, spokesman, So), **Herndon** (on time, on time, on time, time, time). The "'objective' drama" around which the efforts of the Oragean Modernists were focused required a "sacrificial victim" who had to agree to assume that role *consciously.* For that reason, the name "Tod Clifton" is appropriate to this role, since *tod* is the German words for death, and if "Clifton" is read as "cleft" the word may be associated with Michah 1:4. "And the mountains shall be molten under him, and the valleys shall be *cleft*, as wax before the fire, [and] as the waters [that are] poured down a steep place."—a passage that describes the destruction of the world: it is to prevent such a destruction that such extreme measures are called for. Herndon's autobiography is itself unobtrusively "objective" except that its overweening artificiality is in danger of giving it away. Frederick T. Griffiths has no grasp of the esoteric level of the text, so has made a partial assessment of Ellison's appropriation of Herndon:

> [Angelo Herndon's autobiography] *Let Me Live* is, with some telling slips, a remarkably layered performance: Herndon is alarmingly at risk in 1937, but also posturing as a martyr, and in his Angelo-persona suppressing the provocateur "Gene Braxton." As a study in the production and dismantling of martyrdom,

Ellison's Tod Clifton owes much to him. Tod ('death') "plunged out of history" (Invisible 438) (Clifton: 'off a cliff'). In 1937 Herndon was bracketed between his own younger, more reckless self, "Gene Braxton," and the genuine Marxist martyr, older brother Milton. Brother Clifton? The run of names, Clifton/Braxton/Milton, is at least suggestive. Under the mask of Clifton, Ellison gathers Angelo's most glamorous, though hardly unique, fantasies of himself. Like Clifton, the "youth leader" (396), Angelo headed the Young Communists League. The "very black and very handsome" Tod enters with a bandage on his statuesque jaw (363); Herndon tells of being cajoled by the police as "'a good-looking lad'" and "'regular lady-killer'" (Live 107-08) before getting beaten like the Christian Martyrs of old (114). Like Tod, the photogenic Angelo was a sharp dresser, "except his head of Persian lamb's wool had never known a straightener" (*Invisible* 366). Why lamb? Tod ('death') ends up being a sacrificial lamb like Milton; Angelo claims our attention because he might be ("Let me live!"). As discussed above, the label on Tod's zoot suit may read "Negro Quarterly," and his death brings other traces of Angelo to the fore. The historically inaccurate black shirt worn by the policeman who guns down Tod may recall both Angelo's foes, the "American Fascisti Order of the Black Shirts" (Live 165-67) and the Spanish Fascists who shot down Milton. Finally, the invisible man's eulogy for Tod, who "'died like any dog in a road'" (*Invisible* 457), signifies on an embarrassing just-in-case eulogy that Angelo leaves for himself to climax his narrative, proclaiming to an admirer in 1936: "'I would rather die like a man than live like a dog'" (*Live* 332). (Griffiths "Ralph Ellison")

Walter White. Walter White is represented by Jim Trueblood. In this instance irony is ascendant since White, a black civil rights leader, had blond hair and blue eyes and looked like a white person: thus White's blood was not "true." In this instance the name relates to the social level of the text, a practice that is not consistent. White's presence on the social level of the text reverberates against the thematic concern with appearances and purity that comes to the fore in Chapter Ten, when the protagonist finds employment with Liberty Paints. The ten drops of black "dope" that the protagonist drips into the buckets of white paint is a reification of the social construction of blackness due to "one drop" of black blood being sufficient to color a person black: in the case of Walter White the black blood has not determined his appearance. In the Jim Trueblood episode, the word "log" is used for "legominism" and there are many repetitions of the word "white." The text also suggests that a name is being given through phonetic *cabala* since the text says "his name was never mentioned above a whisper" (46). The name is given as "bleached white and warped by the weather" (46)—thus *weather white* sounds the name "Walter White." There is a suggestion that Jim Trueblood also points to the Apostle James, since Trueblood's acceptance of being killed by his wife parallels James's martyrdom:

> Tradition relates that Saint James' martyrdom is the origin of the Catholic understanding of "baptism by blood." The accuser of the Apostle James was so moved by James humility that he was touched by divine grace and desired to die alongside James as a disciple of Jesus Christ. This man received martyrdom along with James the Apostle and the accuser was declared "baptized by blood" and thereby saved and holy. (Marshall "Baptism")

John Hall Wheelock. Like Carl Van Vechten/Mr. Emerson's son, Ellison's physical description of the Mr. Kimbro character is realistic, so that the "stiff military mustache" (194) identifies "Colonel" Kimbro (194) as John Hall Wheelock. Chapter Ten sounds the word "hall" through its fourth, fifth, and sixth paragraphs and the seventh paragraph has the words "locker" "lockers," and "locks" (193). The other elements of the name are more indistinct—"wheel" being sounded by "white hall" (193) and "Well" (194).

Jean Toomer. Toomer's portrayal by the exaggerated Lucius Brockway suggests a familiar theme of the Oragean Modernist movement, that many people found Jean Toomer to be a difficult personality. While this theme has not been explored by scholars, Tolson's important poem *Harlem Gallery* takes Toomer for its protagonist. Tolson's treatment of Toomer-The Curator is not flattering. Tolson uses "tumorous" (ln. 326) to summon Toomer's name in "E. & O. E." Ellison's treatment of Toomer is similarly harsh. Toomer-Brockway is located three levels underground behind a door marked "Danger" (202). In life Toomer was handsome and athletic: Brockway is five feet tall, wiry, and has cottony white hair. That he is Toomer is revealed by the fact that not only does Ellison summon up "Jean" through *"engineer"* (204; Ellison's italics), he alludes to Toomer's complete name, Pinchback, so that he includes *"pine"* (203; Ellison's italics), "machine sounds" (203), a number of uses of "pitch" (203), and Brockway tells the protagonist to "get on *back* up there" (203; emphasis added). "Toomer" is indistinctly given through "metal door marked "Danger"... lit room" (202). It is inescapable that the name "Brockway" was inserted as an indication that Ellison is using phonetic *cabala*, since Brockway so effortlessly suggests "block [the] way." Of course, Brockway is determined to block the way for the protagonist's success, and this parallel between name and action serves to emphasize that there is an element of wordplay in the novel that must be taken into account when evaluating the characters. Toomer's failings as an esotericist are an internal manner and cannot be known beyond the hints given in the Oragean Modernist's novels.

Chapter 3. A Lost Modernism

This is a study of a literary movement. Had the Oragean Modernists failed to publish their writings, there would be nothing to study. From the beginning of the Oragean Modernist movement there had been a close association between esotericism and publishing. In *Gurdjieff's America* P.B. Taylor states that "In effect the intelligentsia of new York—and it was a populous group—was divided into several camps concerning Gurdjieff. One was what I would call the *"New Republic"* group because its editor Herbert Croly and several of its writers became closely associated with Orage" (71-2). Thus, Taylor shows that publishing defined the Oragean Modernist movement from its inception. Other followers of Orage who wrote for the New York Press were John O'Hara Cosgrave, [Gorham] Munson, Frank, Draper, and [T.S.] Matthews, as well as creative writers Zona Gale, Elinor Wylie, Isa Glenn, and Hart Crane. Marjorie Kinnan Rawlings was a journalist in Rochester, New York until 1929. Orage's followers spread through the New York publishing institutions, and as they changed positions their influence increased. T.S. Matthews became the Book editor at *Time.* Gilbert Seldes was managing editor of *The Dial.* Janet Flanner wrote a column for the *New Yorker.*

Far and away the most significant relationships between the Oragean Modernists and publishing were their affiliations with the actual producers of books. It has been said many times that Carl Van Vechten was important to the Harlem Renaissance mostly because he brought the novels of the Harlem writers to Alfred Knopf who published them. Knopf also published Van Vechten's best-selling novels. But never has the subject been broached as to why it was that Knopf was so receptive to those literary works. It is well known that Knopf socialized with Carl Van Vechten. Knopf also published a book by Orage in 1922—*Readers and Writers (1917-1921).* Orage tried to get Knopf to publish Gurdjieff's *Beelzebub's Tales*, but Gurdjieff misbehaved and the deal was never finalized. These few details allow one to make a case for Knopf's having some interest in the Gurdjieff Work. I would go so far as to say that from the esoteric point of view, the Harlem

Renaissance was an esoteric project. Whether or not Alfred Knopf was an esotericist, his willingness to publish the writings of the Oragean Modernists of the Harlem Renaissance generated the so-called Negro fad. The popularity of African-American writing made possible the first phase of the Oragean Modernist program by bringing to the public a considerable collection of esoteric realist texts in popular forms—comic novels, detective stories, and historical novels.

The second phase of the Oragean Modernist publishing program seems to have been centered on the Scribner's publishing house. Scribner's was associated with the most important of the Modernist writers, Hemingway and Fitzgerald. The editors at Scribner's worked with a select group of esoteric writers to gain acclaim for their books. Oragean Modernist writers who published with Scribner's include Dawn Powell, Walter Gilkyson, Marjorie Kinnan Rawlings, and Zora Neale Hurston. Other Oragean Modernist novelists applied to Scribner's but were turned away. Maxwell Perkins worked long and hard with Marjorie Kinnan Rawlings, directing the shaping of her novels until in 1939 her esoteric allegory *The Yearling* won the Pulitzer Prize. The journal *Scribner's* was also an outlet for an outpouring of Oragean Modernist short fiction. (The volume of Oragean Modernist short fiction that was published in the 1920s and 1930s was a torrent, and it suggests that there were followers of Orage on the editorial boards of *Harper's, Atlantic Monthly*, and other such journals.) When I first became aware of Marjorie Kinnan Rawlings's affiliation with the Oragean Modernists, I was surprised by the new information that confronted me. At first it was just that Rawlings had been visited by Zora Neal Hurston. But a closer examination of the Rawlings-Hurston conjunction demonstrated that while Rawlings and Hurston were both Oragean Modernists, they seemed to inhabit separate lines of influence. Thus, when the record of literary history finally shows that Rawlings and Hurston were meeting one another in Florida, there must have already been a long history of Rawlings in some other affiliation with Oragean Modernists other than with Hurston. I examined Rawlings's correspondence with Maxwell Perkins, as I suspected that Perkins and Rawlings were perhaps jointly the key to something, but I was not able to develop anything directly from putting them together. But later research showed that Maxwell Perkins's name turns up in novels by John Dos Passos and Dawn Powell in such a way that it seems that Dos Passos and Powell have identified Perkins as an Oragean Modernist. While Perkins, the most important editor at Scribner's, could not be directly traced to attending A.R. Orage's lectures, two other editors at Scribner's—John Hall Wheelock and Bernice Lesbia Kenyon—could be linked to the Oragean Modernists in multiple and complex ways. Kenyon and her husband Walter Gilkyson published a great deal of esoteric writing, and those two visited Rawlings in Florida beginning in 1940 and maintained a correspondence with her. So, there was a direct linkage established from the Oragean Modernists and Scribner's to Rawlings, though rather late. Since Rawlings began to meet with Hurston about the same time that she became friends with the Gilkysons, there is some suggestion of a realignment among the Oragean Modernists, but there is no telling what that meant in practical terms. Since the Oragean Modernists had no qualms about leaving false trails, there is really no telling what they were doing. Rawlings's correspondence with the Gilkysons establishes when they met her, but this may or may not be true. The same may be said of Rawlings's relationship with Hurston. Given the fact that the archival records of such Oragean Modernists as Ralph Ellison, Melvin Tolson, and Zora Neale Hurston that have been collected in libraries do not reveal their affiliation with the Gurdjieff Work, it is clear that successful attempts have been made to suppress the evidence of their interest in esotericism. Missing are such important pieces of evidence as the extensive drafts of the texts that demonstrate that there was coding involved; similarly, there must have been a huge correspondence among the esotericists that no longer exists. Tellingly, when Ellen Glasgow died, Marjorie Kinnan Rawlings rushed to Richmond and took away her papers saying that she was planning to write a biography of Glasgow. Similar interventions have occurred upon the deaths of several Oragean Modernists—often in the guise of preservation. There are many other indications of the construction of false records, such as

Dawn Powell's diaries and Carl Van Vechten's day books. In both cases these individuals recorded heroic feats of debauchery, while at the same time they were writing prolifically and garnering high critical praise. And we have seen that the writings of the Oragean Modernists often demonstrate a determination to mislead and to misinform the reader who is not on high alert.

There are limits to what outsiders may be able to know about an esoteric group. One of the most important characteristics of the Oragean Modernist project that we must take into account is that they intentionally revealed some portion of their activities in writitings directed to a popular audience. It is uncharacteristic for Western esotericists to have published a large volume of mass market literature as the Oragean Modernists have done. But the reader of these esoteric texts faces the problem of knowing at any time *the nature of what you are reading*. Nowhere is this problem met with more intriguingly than in the case of Zora Neale Hurston: Hurston was trained as an anthropologist, yet wrote as an esotericist. As a result of this practice, her writings have been severely misinterpreted, though it is not the fault of her readers. At the same time, one does wish that Hurston's scholars had been more clever, skeptical, and informed. The entire body of Hurston's writings—anthropology (collections of folklore and essays), short stories published in newspapers, plays written for the WPA, experimental novels, and autobiographies—are esoteric texts. Hurston's texts are only lightly coded, and in many ways they betray their duplicity. Hurston has disguised the esoteric nature of her fictional works by the use of code (the phonetic *cabala* of the alchemists) and by overlaying what she is portraying by the use of distractions—black vernacular, highly figurative and inventive language, and the illusion of black subject matter. To the reader who sees through Hurston's ruses, her texts appear to be cascades of nonsense interspersed with rudimentary esoteric material of an almost banal importance. These qualities make it very difficult to explicate Hurston's writings, particularly when the goal is to gain insight into the operations of the Oragean Modernist esoteric school. But such an inquiry, carried out successfully is particularly informative.

One of Hurston's most controversial books is *Mules and Men*. One of the familiar features of Hurston scholarship is the repeated theme of confusion that scholars have expressed at every turn, and even the title of *Mules and Men* has elicited comments about its meaning. Harold Bloom says that "Hurston's ambiguous title captures the richness of her analysis" (*Zora Neale Hurston* 125). Taking in considerably more of the text, Jacqueline Fulmer observes that "With a similar sense of ambuguity, *Mules and Men* ends with Hurston comparing herself to Sis Cat, who fools and eats Rat by using her "manners," i.e., washing her face after dinner" (*Folk Women* 59). Indeed, upon examination, one does notice that *Mules and Men* is an odd title. It is meant to be odd; in fact it is meant to produce a reaction that will ultimately lead the reader to decode it: *Mules and Men* is phonetic *cabala* for "mend man's soul," a phrase that might be meaningless outside of the context of the Gurdjieff Work. But since the Work assumes that man has no "soul," it is soon realized that the idea of "mending" is merely shorthand, and that another way of saying this is to assert that the "soul" must be healed rather than to say that it must be supplied. The radical nature of the proposition that man has no soul must be recognized, since most people believe that there is a soul and the soul is both wounded and immortal. In the Work even when the soul is gained, it may not be immortal. Hurston's title does not urge an esoteric idea, but conforms to conventional doctrines about the soul. But perhaps this is the best that Hurston can do in a three word title that addresses an elaborate and arcane metaphysics:

> [L]ike most Theosophists, Gurdjieff calls the 4th body *soul*. It is the *soul* Gurdjieff's "Work" is all about. But, equally ironic, in his version of thanatology Gurdjieff (not unequivocally) radically departs both from traditional wisdom doctrines and Theosophy: if not worked upon sufficiently and not awakened, even *soul* is mortal. It is "eaten by the Moon"— probably the weirdest destiny that has ever befallen the spiritual element in man. So, in his rather incongruous blend of

Theosophy, Neopythagoreanism, Rosicrucianism and Alchemy, even (in a few interpretations, the inborn spiritual self is doomed to post-mortem extinction in ordinary human beings. (Harvat "Gurdjieff"; emphases in original text)

Mules and Men opens with an episode in which Hurston is taken to a "toe party." Hurston does not know what a "toe party" is, a revelation that like the title has elicited comments from Hurston scholars, since the whole premise of her folklore collecting activity is that she is a native of the central Florida region. K. Benedicto observes that Hurston's expertise was thin given that she was never previously an adult in Eatonville: "The only insight into the adult culture of Eatonville occurs at the toe party, and Zora's ignorance of what a toe party is reflects her exclusion from adult culture" ("*Mules and Men*: Food, Secrets, Inclusion."). This supposition is doubly absurd. We have already seen that in her essay "Characteristics" Hurston maintains that there are no secrets. Now Benedicto asserts that there are secrets about things that do not need to be kept secret. How would a native of the region, even a child, not be aware of an adult activity of such shining innocence as the toe party?

The premise of the toe party is that men choose their dates by purchasing a woman's toe, and are then obligated to treat her to whatever she might enjoy. The sale of toes repeats several times throughout the evening. This gathering ensures everyone mixes and mingles with many different partners and levels the playing field. The curtain separating the genders removes the hierarchy of attraction from the social interaction, though some fellows "ungallantly ran out the door" [15]. (Benedicto "Food")

This social activity is more childish than "spin the bottle." And it is hard to see why the hiding of women behind a curtain in any way "levels the playing field"—since the men not only choose the women but can (and do) run away. Now, if the roles were reversed and the women got a chance to choose their partners, and to run away, that might be leveling the playing field. So, we have to wonder at the authenticity of this game: did anyone ever actually have a "toe party"? It seems more likely that this is another case of a "lawful inexactitude" than an actual event. Furthermore, no other account of a "toe party" has emerged from my research into Florida folklore. No only that, but if we compare the "toe party" to what goes on in the jook joint in a later chapter of *Mules and Men*, we have to wonder whether the black society in existence in Florida in 1930 would be able to overcome their tendencies toward, possessiveness, chauvinism, jealousy, and the ethos of "badness" to be able to behave as they did in Hursrton's account of the "toe party": I doubt it. (See Adam Gussow's comments on Hurston and "juke-joint aggression" in *Seems Like Murder Here* 15.)

What then is being described in the "toe party" episode? It is the dramatization of the phrase—*Toe the party line.* If we substutute a political context for the folk context, the episode makes perfect sense. Hurston wishes to depict an activity that is consistent on its own terms. "To toe the pary line" means to behave in accordance with the doctrines of the CPUSA—the Communist Party. In this regard Charlie Post shows the relevance of the concept when he states that

> Once the leadership of the Comintern and the CPUSA consolidated their new popular front strategy during the summer of 1936, the room for CP worker militants to pursue the short-lived united front policy was radically reduced. CP unionists who wanted to remain in the party, or who hoped to ascend to union office or a staff job in the new industrial unions, would *"toe the line"* or face disciplinary action. ("The Comintern"; emphasis addded)

But while lining up their toes with party discipline, the party-members at Hurston's metaphorical "toe party" are hidden behind a curtain. Hurston is at pains to show that they have a hidden agenda. In other words this is Hurston's portryal of the manner in which the Oragean Modernists joined the CPUSA in order to carry out their own program. While the idea that anyone would do this seems outrageous, we must recall that such a program was hinted at in *Infants of the Spring* by Wallace Thurman—another Oragean Modernist: "And if out of a wholesale allegiance to Communism the Negro could develop just a half dozen men who were really and truly outstanding the result would be worth the effort" (*Infants* 219). We must recall that an esotericist wrote and disseminated the previous statement, for *Infants of the Spring* is an esoteric novel. Thurman's declaration about the utility of Communism for engendering supermen requires some adjustment before it can be understood properly: what it leaves out is that the abstraction "the Negro" is not a social entity that was programmatically concerned with developing outstanding men. The entity that had such a concern was the esoteric school that followed A.R. Orage. Orage's school, then, would have to arrange for a cadre of esotericists to join the CPUSA and then to covertly recruit from the membership of the party in order to develop those individuals capable of taking on the Gurdjieff Work. In this way the CPUSA would supply the personnel and the covering organization within which supermen would be fostered. And this is exactly what Hurston's "toe party" episode is saying, that such a program had been put into practice by the Oragean Modernists.

The infiltration of the CPUSA that was projected by Wallace Thurman in *Infants of the Spring* was but a component of a larger scheme that Orage's followers would use to save the planet Earth from an imminent destruction. This scheme was described to some extent in C. Daly King's presentation of Fourth Way doctrines, *The Oragean Version*. The plan was to use the CPUSA as the medium through which to stage an "'Objective' drama" that would have a far-reaching effect on world history. In effect the Oragean Modernists would re-enact the drama of Jesus the Christ—but it was important to understand that for the Oragean Modernists the Christ–drama was itself a re-enactment of a far more ancient Horus-Osiris drama by Egyptian esotericists in a far earlier period:

About us, in the creeds, the sects and the distortions of modern Christianity lay the fragments, of another work of Objective Art, the life of Christ, so it has been said. According to that account the story of the Christ, a messenger of God upon this planet, was and is Objective Drama, played not on a stage but in life by the Essene initiate, Jesus. This play had its origin far earlier, in ancient Egypt, as the drama of the life, death and resurrection of Ausar (Osiris), the God-in-Man; its function was to present ultimate human truths through the medium of consciously acted roles. For centuries, we are told, the later Essene brotherhood, a School itself deriving from Egyptian origins, had held the aim of presenting this drama in life rather than as a prescribed mystery play and for generations had trained its postulants to that end. Eventually the cast of thirteen was complete with Jesus, who had been sent to Egypt for temple training there, cast as the leading actor and Judas, who must play the next most difficult role, that of the betrayer, fully prepared for his part. With the necessary modifications demanded by the local scene and times, the action began. (King, 163-64)

We have seen that in *Invisible Man* Ralph Ellison presents Zora Neale Hurston as Mary Rambo. The name "Mary" points to her role in the Objective Drama of Christ, and the "womb" suggests the Egyptian element of the drama. This assignment is even confirmed by Dawn Powell in *The Locusts Have No King*, where she says: "The two gentlemen strolled amiably arm-in-arm away from the center of chatter, pausing to consider a huge Zorach marble mother-and-child on the landing flanked by massive urns of chrysanthemums" (20). The sentence both gives Hurston's name in the phonetic *cabala* and refers to her role as the Madonna. Not only are two of Hurston's novels esoteric, they are thinly veiled retellings of the story of Isis, Osiris, and Horus: *Their Eyes Were Watching God* and *Seraph of the Suwanee* are intricately informed by the Egyptology of Gerald Massey, who like the Orageans also believed that the Christ-drama was derived from the religion of Horus. Hurston's Rambo / "womb" name recapitulates the idea that the ankh—the Egyptian symbol of life—depicts the *womb* of Isis. There is little doubt that Hurston played the role of the Mother in the objective drama of the Oragean Modernists. The mystery that remains is why in particular Hurston was given that role, and how she might have carried it out through esoteric activity. Finally, it remains to be established how the fifteen-years that Hurston's spent writing a novel about Herod related to her maternal role in the "'objective' drama."

Barbara Foley's study of the earlier drafts of Ralph Ellison's novel, *Invisible Man*, show that in the published version of the novel, the significance of Mary Rambo has been obscured: Foley states that

> No section of *Invisible Man* underwent more rewriting than the chapters depicting the protagonist's hospital experience and subsequent encounter with Mary Rambo: material occupying little more than twenty pages in the published text ran to several hundred handwritten and typewritten manuscript pages. (Kindle Locations 2848-2849)

The revising first involved a former tenant of Mary Rambo's, a deceased merchant sea-man, who the editor's at Knopf wanted Ellison to omit because he took up a great deal of space but was not present in the narrative. Foley was not aware that Mary Rambo is a portrayal of Hurston; nor was she aware of the esoteric level of *Invisible* Man. To compensate for the importance of Mary Rambo and LeRoy to Ellison, Foley discusses them as expressions of Ellison's interest in "the Cambridge School scholars and their Marxist descendents" (Kindle location 1187). It is evident that this character relates to the esoteric level of the text, where he serves as part of the Christ-drama:

> Down to his chosen name (in old French LeRoy means "the king"), Ellison's heroic mariner is recognizable,

albeit in twentieth-century African American guise, as an avatar of the dying king or god described by Frazer, Raglan, and the Cambridge School. Like Raglan's hero, he knows nothing of his parents, travels to another land, does great deeds, is honored as a king, then falls out of favor with the gods and meets with a mysterious death. Like the dying gods of ancient myth, whose bodies were "torn in pieces, scattered over the fields, lost, sought for, discovered and recognized," LeRoy is the classic *sparagmos*. The purple wreath and flowers, signifying his royal status, associate him with Adonis of Greek myth; his death by water links him with both Osiris, the Nile god, and Dionysus. Occurring in the fall, LeRoy's death, like that of the year-daimon, is aligned with cyclical patterns of death and rebirth; the cubist portrait featuring the hanged man in the corner has replaced Harvest Home, with its gathered abundance amid the "blood-red leaves." At the feast memorializing his death and celebrating his life, LeRoy is ritually consumed as the animal totem "King Tom." Along with cubism, the hanged god has come to Harlem. (Kindle Locations 3079-3083).

Under tremendous pressure from his editor, Ellison relented and removed LeRoi from his text. The importance of Mary Rambo to the esoteric plan of the novel is demonstrated by Ellison's refusal to remove her from his manuscript:

Aware of the centrality of LeRoy to the entire rooming house episode, [Knopf editor Harry] Ford observed, "If LeRoy goes, then it seems to me that Mary has no reasons for being, and all passages relevant should be deleted. I would see this as an invaluable tightening of the narrative, which is much too loose and shifty from here on." Ellison eventually chopped apart his novel, tossing [the other tenant's rooming with Mary Rambo] Mrs. Garfield, Portwood, Cleo, and Mary into folders from which Mary alone, in dismembered form, would emerge. (Kindle Locations 3266-3268).

Ellison compensated for the removal of LeRoi by making Tod Clifton his "dying god," but he could not compensate for the removal of Hurston-Mary Rambo, and so in spite of fierce opposition he retained her in the final form of the novel. Finally, we must note that "in postpublication commentaries Ellison continually denied that the Brotherhood is the cp" (Foley Kindle Locations 3288-3291). Foley argues that Ellison's assertion does not matter, for she sees that the behavior of the Brotherhood irrefutably models that of the CPUSA. But *Invisible Man* is an esoteric novel, and the Brotherhood is not the CPUSA; the Brotherhood is the Institute for the Harmonious Development of Man, the dark side—so to speak— of the Fourth Way school, and the arrogant, doctrinaire leader, Brother Jack, is Gurdjieff in disguise.

Hurston, like Ellison, also framed the "objective" Christ-drama in a work of fiction, and it is expressly with Herod Antipas, a historical figure connected to the story of Jesus Christ, that both writers converge. In the published text of *Invisible Man* Tod Clifton serves as the sacrificial victim, and when Clifton is killed by the police "even the familiar woman street preacher was shouting a sermon about *the slaughter of the innocents*" (Chapter 23, emphasis added). In the conventional reading of the Bible, Herod is a villain, and he is closely associated with the attempt to murder the messiah known as "the slaughter of the innocents." For the last ten years of her life, Hurston wrote a historical novel about Herod Antipas. Since Hurston scholars do not recognized that Hurston was an esotericist, it has been difficult for them to integrate the unpublished novel, *Herod*, into her corpus, as Michael Lackey's review of Deborah Plant's book makes clear: "… Hurston's *Herod* challenges the New Testament version of the baby-murdering tyrant by suggesting that he was actually a forerunner of Christ… Original in thought, she had to be bold in spirit as she created a work that defied history" (Lackey 142). Missing the Oragean connection, Plant cannot convincingly explain why Herod is "Hurston's ideal individual" (Lackey 142). Hurston's unfinished novel "Herod" was based on the Oragean belief that two thousand years ago Essene esotericists had intervened in history. Gerald Massey—a source of much of Hurston's biblical lore— denied that Herod carried out the slaughter of the innocents:

> The massacre of the Innocents is a common legend. In the Jewish traditions there is a massacre of the little ones at the time of Moses' birth, in which the Pharaoh plays the part of the monster Herod. So universal was this murder that no distinction was made betwixt the children of the Egyptians and the Jews. On the day that Moses was born the astrologers told Pharaoh they had seen in the stars that the deliverer of the Jews had been born that day, but they could not tell whether his parents were Egyptian or Jewish. Therefore Pharaoh kills not only all the Jewish boys born that day, but also all the Egyptians (for authorities see *Proceedings of the Society of Biblical Archaeology*, December 4, 1888). It is the old, old story of the child that was born to be king in defiance of all obstacles. (Massey "The Jesus-Legend in Rome")

Moreover, Gurdjieff and Massey shared the idea that ancient Egypt was the source of Christianity: "In the Appendix to *Ancient Egypt*, Massey listed more than 200 direct parallels between the Jesus legend and the cycle of Osiris/Horus. The earthly Jesus is congruent to Horus; Jesus the Christ corresponds to Osiris, the resurrected god" (Finch "IV the Natural Genesis" *Nile Genesis*).

Throughout Melvin B. Tolson's epic poem about the Harlem Renaissance, he uses the phrase "life and art"—as in

"Life and Art," said Doctor Nkomo, "beget incestuously
(like Osiris and Isis)
the talented of brush and pen.
Artistic instinct draws,
on a rock in the Kalahari Desert,

a crocodile for Bush-born men.
Without Velasquez and Cranach,
what would Picasso be?"
(*Harlem Gallery*)

While it is tempting to think that the importance of "life and art" is figurative, conjectural, and philosophical, it seems foolhardy, since Tolson was another of the Oragean Modernist conspirators. The troubled relationship between life and art to which Tolson alludes is contextualized by the esoteric practice of creating works of "objective" art in history through the employment of "conscious actors." According to Orage, the Essenes had previously intervened in history through the "objective" work of art that consisted of the events that surrounded Jesus the messiah. It was the intention of the Oragean Modernists to enact a similar work of "objective art" in modern times through the unwitting agency of the CPUSA. The plan was to capitalize on the "martyrdoms" of Angelo Herndon who played a conscious role in the drama), and the Scottsboro Nine (who were innocent of any awareness of the "objective" drama).

There is no straightforward account of this esoteric "historical" activity. What exists is a fragmentary record that may be assembled from literary texts. This reconstruction is possible because *the Oragean Modernists were never one-dimensional in the construction of their texts: there is always an encoded content, so it is always possible to learn something about their ideas and concerns.* We have already seen that in describing her "toe party" Hurston points to the esotericists hidden in the CPUSA, and that Ellison's confusing conflation of the Brotherhood and the CP also is a disguise for the Oragean Modernist's political–historical conspiracy. A number of other elements may be added to this list.

Melvin Tolson called himself a Marxist and claimed to have organized tenant farmers in Texas. In the 1930s he wrote a social-realist epic poem, *A Gallery of Harlem Portraits*; however, he was not able to find a commercial publisher due to the poem's politically radical content. This long poem was written in a simple style that disallowed complex ciphers, so Tolson encrypted the strange names that he used for his characters, and thus his table of contents was used to construct a coded text. At one point in the table of contents Tolson uses the name "Aunt Tommizene" to say that he is "not a Communist"—or more exactly—"ain't Commie." This demonstrates that not only did the Oragean Modernists align themselves with the left, they worked very hard to simulate leftist literary works. It is no mean feat to produce a book-length epic poem like *A Gallery of Harlem Portraits*. But how much more difficult it must have been for Tolson to fabricate a credibly revolutionary epic poem that carried an esoteric subtext. So authentically insurgent was his poem, that it was unpublishable by the commercial presses of the 1930s. And yet the poem covertly reveals that its politics are inauthentic and that it is an esoteric text.

Dorothy West, a novelist and short story writer in the Harlem Renaissance became more even prominent in the 1930s:

> In 1931, West joined a large group of African-American writers and artists who traveled to the Soviet Union to make a film about race in different cultures. Though the film was never made, West remained in the Soviet Union for a year. She spent some of that time traveling with another member of the film group, the poet Langston Hughes. …
>
> After her return to the United States, West became the founding editor of *The Challenge*, a magazine devoted to publishing the best writing by African Americans. When the publication failed, West founded and edited *The New Challenge*, maintaining her commitment to publishing new writing by African Americans. (Web.)

The Challenge was an Oragean Modernist literary journal disguised as a leftist journal. West's journal published esotericists posing as Marxists, such as Ralph Ellison, Margaret Walker, Arna Bontemps, Pauli Murray, Mae Cowdery, and Waring Cuney. "Challenge" was a cipher that used the phoentic *cabala* to say "all in G." This proposition was not true, since the journal necessarily published writers who were not involved in the esoteric. Among the non-esoteric works published in the journal was Richard Wright's groundbreaking essay "Blueprint for Negro Writing." Wests's first novel *The Living Is Easy* (1948) was esoteric and written using the phonetic *cabala*. But when West traveled to the Soviet Union and lived there for a while, the published accounts of her experiences were also esoteric and encrypted with Gurdjieffian material. Here is the second paragraph of her account of her stay in Moscow, "Room in Red Square":

> There is only one way to go to Russia. Not as a tourist, paying voluta, which is the hallowed name for foreign currency, and seeing Muscovite behavior from those amazing Lincolns that stand outside the bourgeois hotels, manned by the most reckless chauffeurs in the world, and interpreters intelligent enough to show the gaping, gory-minded foreigners Russia in her summer frock of picturesque peasant in his smock and straw shoes, and city worker in his park of culture and rest. (10)

The passage is rhetorical nonsense. Inserted within the random, anarchic contents are the syllables that sound out the "hallowed name[s']" of Orage and Gurdjieff through the phonetic *cabala*: "bourgeois- foreigners-tourist- picturesque" accumulate to "Orage," and "gory-chauffeurs," is an approximation of "Gurdjieff" in line with what has been seen in other Oragean Modernist texts.

Louise Thompson Patterson [Aaron Douglas, Augusta Savage]. Louise Thompson Patterson was a minor figure in the Harlem Renaissance but a major figure in the 1930s. Thompson had been married to Wallace Thurman, whose novels reveal him as a major theorist of the Oragean Modernist intervention in history. Thompson figures prominently in discussions of the political left in Harlem in the 1930s. She was not a writer and she was not directly identifiable as having been a follower of A.R. Orage, so in many ways she is a difficult figure to deal with. When Langston Hughes and Zora Neale Hurston collaborated on the musical play, *Mule Bone*, Thompson served as their secretary.

Louise Thompson serves as a transitional figure between the Harlem Renaissance and the Oragean Modernist "objective" drama in which there was an infiltration of the CPUSA and an intervention in history. Thompson was the most important figure in turning the Harlem group towards the left through her film project that took many black artists to the Soviet Union. (It must be emphasized that Langston Hughes was not an esotericist. Even though Hughes worked closely with Louise Thompson, there seems to have been a deception at work where Hughes had no grasp of the real activities of the Oragean Modernists. Hughes's status is in no way ambiguous, for the Oragean Modernits inserted many indications into their texts that Hughes was an outsider.) Jack El-Hai, explaining that Thompson was restless with the complacency of the Harlem scene and wanted to effect major social changes, provides this "exoteric" account of Thompson's activities in 1932:

> One day opportunity arrived in the person of James W. Ford, a prominent African-American communist. Just returned from Russia, he showed Thompson a letter from the Meschrabpom Film company of Moscow. The Soviets planned to make a film titled *Black and White*, about Negro life in the United States, and it needed an African-American cast. Ford asked Thompson to organize the trip and to go along herself.
>
> A master manager, Thompson recruited sponsors and supporters and typed countless letters. "Hollywood producers continue to manufacture sentimental and banal pictures, and particularly cling to traditional types in portraying the Negro," ran one such appeal for the project. "At such a time, *Black and White*, produced under the best directive experience of Russia, comes as a pictorial event of the greatest artistic and social significance."
>
> By the start of June 1932, an eclectic group of 22 would-be actors had signed on. It included students, social workers, three experienced actors, journalists, a

postal worker, and even a paperhanger. Most important to Thompson, however, the group included Langston Hughes. Eager to have a close friend along, she had pleaded with him to come.

On June 14 the group settled aboard the ship *Europa*. Hughes, lugging a phonograph and collection of jazz records, was the last to board. Thompson already knew this journey would prove more than just a pleasure trip. "We were told," she later wrote, "that there was no racism practiced in the Soviet Union.... This was something new under the sun."

Once the *Europa* launched, the behavior of some of her fellows worried Thompson. Ted Poston, a reporter, and Thurston Lewis, an actor with minor stage credits, "have been thoroughly irresponsible," she wrote of their constant skirt-chasing. "Their actions have shamed us all, for they have acted like puppies, chained for a while and then released." Another newsman, Henry Lee Moon, later upset Thompson by joining in the disruptiveness.

Arrived in Moscow, they learned that Russian writers were still working on the *Black and White* screenplay. So the Americans had plenty of free time. From the comfort of the Grand Hotel, near the Kremlin, Thompson explored the city with Hughes and his friends Loren Miller and Matt Crawford.

"Everywhere we go we are treated as honored guests, given enthusiastic ovations, and offered the best," she wrote to her mother. The group was seated in the presidium for a Moscow celebration of Constitution Day, attended a reception for the Bolshoi Ballet, and spent evenings listening to a terrible jazz ensemble in the Hotel Metropole bar.

Meanwhile, the group met the film's German director, Karl Junghans, and other Meschrabpom officials. The Russians puzzled over the Americans. "Russians, as do most Europeans, ... think Negro means literally black, and our group has been the subject of much discussion on this point," Thompson wrote. "We have had to argue at great lengths to tell them that we are all Negroes, and to try to explain just what being a Negro means in the United States."

Hughes had finally read an English version of the script and saw problems. Set in Birmingham, Alabama, the story focused on black steel workers suffering under exploitation by their white bosses. Hughes pronounced the script fatally flawed by many absurdities: a rich white Alabaman asking a black woman to dance; a black-owned network of radio stations; and, in the finale, the arrival of the Red Army to rout the hired goons of the industrialists. The Russians promised to fix it.

By mid-July, no revision had appeared, and the group grew bored and restless. Meschrabpom prescribed a vacation at the Black Sea, after which the filming could start. They took a train to the welcoming beaches of Odessa.

Soon a Meschrabpom official arrived to break bad news: For lack of a usable script, there would be no production of *Black and White* in 1932. With this announcement, internal conflicts reopened. In a letter to home, Thompson wrote that a few of the group said "that we have been betrayed and that all the Negro people in the world have been betrayed." U.S. reporters in Moscow had spread rumors that an American engineer helping the Russians with massive construction projects had advised Josef Stalin to abandon *Black and White.* The dissenters of the group believed that the Soviets, desperate for official political recognition by the U.S., had cancelled the film to mollify the capitalists.

Returned to Moscow, Thompson made the case that their hosts were merely disorganized and should be given the benefit of the doubt. The dissenters thought the Meschrabpom defenders were naïve.

Finally the group went before the Comintern, the governing body of worldwide communism, to lay out each faction's opinion. Thompson and her followers urged the Comintern not to further delay shooting. The dissidents accused the Russians of kowtowing to the U.S. government and proving their enmity to the black race. Undoubtedly taken aback, the communist officials returned a judgment "that Meschrabpom had been very inefficient and that an investigation would be made," Thompson wrote.

In the meantime, the group could go home, look for work in the U.S.S.R., or accept a theatrical trade union's offer of a six-week tour of Soviet Asia. Thompson and most of the rest signed up for the tour of Asia, though Hughes planned to leave the tour partway through.

Thompson expected that the tour would be the greatest experience of her life, but as she prepared to leave, she received word that her mother was very ill. Agonized, she made her choice with her mother's blessing: Thompson joined the tour. She never regretted the decision.

She returned to New York on November 17, 1932, to find her mother still living, though they had only three months together.

Meschrabpom promised to resume production of *Black and White* the following summer. Someone (possibly Thompson) did revise the English film script to eliminate the worst absurdities. But Meschrabpom ultimately gave up on the movie.

The effort to make *Black and White*, though quickly forgotten, catapulted its participants to high achievement. By gathering this group and dropping them into Russia's radicalizing stew, this never-made picture changed the course of U.S. history. Loren Miller, politically charged in Russia, became an attorney who argued against racially restrictive housing covenants before the U.S. Supreme Court and later sat as a California Superior Court Justice. Dorothy West enjoyed an extraordinary literary career as the author of *The Living Is Easy, The*

Wedding, and many stories and essays. Frank Montero campaigned for integration and became associate executive director of the National Urban League. Homer Smith served as the only African-American reporter on World War II's eastern front. And Langston Hughes, who often referred to his Soviet journey in his writings, was one of the best-known figures of the Harlem Renaissance. (El-Hai "Reel Life)

Examined from the esoteric perspective, Louise Thompson's activities and motivations have an entirely different meaning. What Thompson was doing may be thought of as the "Sovietization" of the Oragean Modernist "objective" drama. By merging the Oragean Modernist narrative with the *Black and White* film project and by establishing themselves in the Soviet Union, the Oragean Modernists established impeccable credentials as leftists. It cannot be emphasized sufficiently that it was Louise Thompson who was at the center of this transformation from Harlem aestheticism to leftist agitation. Joy G. Carew states that "Organizer Thompson had assured them that they would be reimbursed once they got to the Soviet Union, but they still had to put forth their money first" (116). Thompson's success at enrolling a cadre of young people in her film project is the historical analogue to what Hurston describes allegorically in her description of bringing in a haul of "shrimp" (see below) in her novel *Seraph on the Suwanee*:

Black and White was to be a major Soviet propaganda film that would show the American Negro "in his true character" and expose the evils of racism. The story, situated at a steel mill in the American South, would demonstrate the solidarity between white and black workers overcoming the most draconian of situations. It was to "be a departure from the traditional pattern [and trace] the development of the Negro people in America, their work, their play, their progress, their difficulties-devoid of sentimentality as well as of buffoonery" The film was sure to be welcomed "by discriminating patrons of the cinema and those people sincerely interested in the Negro." All the official Black and White film members were black, save one, Allen McKenzie. Six of them, Hughes, Wayland Rudd, Juanita Lewis, Thurston McNairy Lewis, Dorothy West, and Estelle Winwood, had previous experience in the theater. Most, save Hughes, Smith, Louise Thompson, and one or two others, had no formal political agenda. Most were temporary sojourners, glad to be going for their contracted time; and some were secretly hoping to find ways to stay on. Noted Hughes, "[The] two professionals [Rudd and Winwood] were also the only real mature people in our group, everyone else being well under thirty and some hardly out of their teens ... an art student just out of Hampton, teacher, a girl elocutionist from Seattle, three would-be writers other than myself, a very pretty divorcee who traveled on alimony, a female swimming instructor, and various clerks and stenographers" Smith noted, "They came from such distances as California, Minnesota and even Montego Bay, Jamaica.... Wayland Rudd, who had worked in 'Porgy'; Taylor Gordon, writer and concert singer; Loren Miller, now a prominent Los Angeles attorney; Ted R. Poston, New York newsman; and Henry Lee Moon, prominent publicist and author, were amongst the twenty-two" Faith Berry's list was the most comprehensive: Lawrence O. Alberga, an agricultural worker; Matthew Crawford, an insurance clerk; Sylvia Garner, a singer and actress; social workers Constance White, Katherine Jenkins, and Leonard Hill; George Sample, a law student and Jenkins's fiance; Mildred Jones, an art student; Juanita Lewis, a singer; Mollie Lewis, a graduate student; Thurston McNairy Lewis, an actor; Allen McKenzie, a salesman; Frank C. Montero, a student; Henry Lee Moon, a reporter; Lloyd Patterson, a paperhanger and artist; Theodore R. Poston, a reporter; Wayland Rudd, an actor; Neil Homer Smith, a postal clerk and journalist; and Dorothy West, a writer and actress. Although several of the participants had the last name Lewis, Berry did not indicate whether any of them were relatives. 'Two of them, McKenzie and Rudd, were also known to have white female traveling companions.' (Carew 115-15)

Returning from the Soviet Union, Thompson joined with other Oragean Modernists in organizing art organizations with a left political agenda:

> As the Depression devastated Harlem, Thompson joined with the African American sculptor, Augusta Savage, to form the Vanguard, a radical artists group in opposition to those within the Harlem Renaissance who continued to seek the traditional path of finding wealthy patrons and gaining entry into establishment institutions. Attracted also to both the committed anti-racism and socialism of the Soviet revolution, she organized the Harlem branch of the American Friends of the Soviet Union and began to study Marxism at the CPUSA's Workers' School.

> In 1932, she organized and led a group of Black artists, including Langston Hughes and her former husband, Wallace Thurman, to the Soviet Union to produce a film about African American life and struggles for liberation. Although the film was not made, the excursion was viewed positively by Thompson and most of the other artists. (Markowitz "Mountain Top")

What is particularly of note in discussing the interface of the radical left and esotericism is the persistent tendency of the Oragean Modernists to present their activities in such a way that they may be discovered to be esotericists. In the case of the Vanguard salon, Aaron Douglas designed a cover for a journal that was never published. The journal, "Spark, Organ of the Vanguard" not only offers the names of Orage and Gurdjieff in the phonetic *cabala*, it contains an instance of wordplay: if "spark" is reversed, it says "crap," an indication that the affiliation of the organization's leading figures was inauthentic—merely another episode of role playing. Aaron Douglas, one of the few Gurdjieffians who did not hide his esoteric interests, always maintained that his works of art were not influenced by esoteric ideas. Douglas's statement has been taken at face value by Douglas's scholars Amy *Kirschke* and Marissa Vincenti due to their unfamiliarity with esoteric ideas. It is not difficult to see that Douglas's paintings are permeated with esoteric information. But in the case of the cover that he designed for the Vanguard salon, the design presents political iconography superimposed on the enneagram, the symbol most associated with Gurdjieff (see Chapter 14 *of In Search of the Miraculous* by P.D. Ouspensky). Once the design has been understood, the real meaning of Hurston's "toe party" may be seen at first hand—for in this case the Oragean Modernists were hiding behind their most important symbol:

In the figure above, Douglas has lined up the number six (6) on the enneagram with the number six (6) that appears to be a link of chain in his illustration. In the figure below, it is shown that Douglas's design incorporated at least two enneagrams in order to arrive at the complex cubist geometry that form his arresting graphic design.

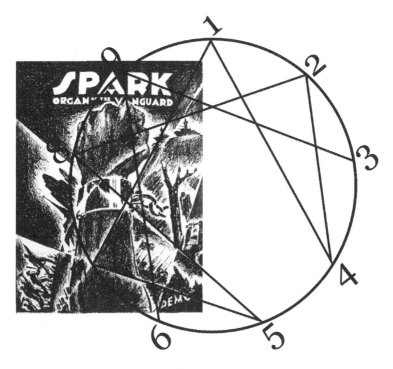

In effect the whole of the Oragean Modernist project was a matter of recruitment. If sufficient "food" were sent to the Moon, the Earth would be saved. The problem was that such "food"—the vibrations derived from the higher sort of individuals was difficult to produce. While recruitment is not absent from Ellison's treatment of esotericism in *Invisible Man*, the theme is muddled. Zora Neale Hurston addresses the subject of recruitment directly in her novel, *Seraph on the Suwanee.* The process of recruitment is presented as shrimp fishing. The narrative seems to be a closely-observed and realistic description of shrimp fishing in Florida waters; beneath the surface there is a running account of the Gurdjieff school in America. The text is a running catalogue of coded material; Hurston marks these instances of *legominisms* with phrases such as "Let's get it" (224, 335) and "Let go my husband's leg!" (329). The first lowering of the fishing net produces an inadequate harvest:

> Turtles, numerous kinds of fish, a leopard shark, strange unimaginable-shaped things from the bottom of the sea cascaded out on the deck. Things in shells, soft-looking queer-shaped things; four octopi, about four feet across, bent their arms like swastikas and rolled about the deck trying to find their way back to the water. Jim stood with his hands on his hips looking down gloomily on the mass. Plenty of stuff, but few shrimp in all that mass. (335-6)

The passage is a description of Gurdjieff's visit to New York in 1924; "Turtles, numerous kinds of fish" is [Jean] Toomer's name, and the octopi are the performers of the sacred dances that so interested New Yorker's in Gurdjieff's school. The octopi were used to represent the dancers because the movements were based on the "Law of Eight," and the swastika effect is literal, as the photo below demonstrates:

Hurston next describes the purge of Ouspensky: "Arvay saw several things that looked to her like living *pin cushions* and thought to get one to save and take home with her" (336; emphasis added). Next Gurdjieff is purged; he is rightly depicted as a shark since one of the most famous things ever said about him was Wyndham Lewis's quip that he was a "Levantine psychic shark" (Mistlberger 253), and Hurston has memorialized this by making the shark specifically a "leopard shark" (335),—the scientific name of which, *Triakis semifasciata*, offers a play on words suggestive of "a tricky fascist." Gurdjieff's murder is elaborately imagined:

> The men went in killing things. First that astonishingly limber-bodied shark. It could whip its body around as if it hadn't a bone in it. With shovels and the axe, they fell upon it cursing the whole shark family as improperly born cutters of nets, and hefted it overside, where it was immediately fallen upon by other sharks and disappeared in a few minutes down their under-slung, saw-toothed mouths. (336)

In the interlude between harvests the name "Angelo Herndon" is presented; the passage provides directions for reading the encoded names—to proceed in both directions and to listen to the *sounds*:

> There was an old coverless *Adventure* magazine on the table beside the head of the bunk, and Arvay picked it up and tried to read it some. All she did was to turn pages from front to back and then the other way. She looked out of first one window and then another, at the peaceful, waving horizon, at the distant boats circling and circling around flags. She could tell when the nets were taken on board by the swarms of birds and their hungry, unmusical cries. (337)

The following paragraph roughly sounds out the name "Patterson," the next sounds out "Augusta," the penultimate paragraph on page 337 sounds "Louise, and the final paragraph contains the word "savage:" if the names are combined in the correct order they give the names of the directors of the Vanguard and other Harlem cultural organizations—Augusta Savage and Louise Thompson [Patterson]. Louise Thompson Patterson's talents as an organizer and public speaker drew her into the battle in 1932 to save the Scottsboro Nine, African American youths framed up on rape charges in Alabama. After 1933, she worked for the National Committee for the Defense of Political Prisoners, serving as assistant national secretary. She also officially joined the Communist Party. Patterson organized several Harlem events and a march on the nation's capital to protest the plight of the Scottsboro defendants, which succeeded in blocking their execution. Later Savage and Thompson worked on behalf of Angelo Herndon.

The "shrimp" that are hauled in on the final casting of the net in *Seraph on the Suwanee* is the crowd of 6,000 well-wishers at Pennsylvania Station in New York City that greeted Herndon on his return to New York after two years in prison in Georgia. Herndon had been imprisoned for "insurrection" after being caught in possession of Communist propaganda tracts in 1932. Angelo Herndon is put forward by Ellison and Hurston as a figure playing a conscious role in the Oragean Modernist "objective" drama. *Let Me Live*, the title of his esoteric autobiography, does not seem to be a case of the phonetic *cabala*, but seems instead to use the *lamed vau* formula so that the word "live" includes the letters lv that in Hebrew are the number 36: —36 / lv—to indicate that Herndon thought that he was one of the "inner circle of humanity," one of the *tzadikim.* This lv formula was used by Melvin Tolson throughout his published poetry, as in a line about esoteric schools,"as they present to the wolves" (*Harlem Gallery* "Omicron"). The idea is that the "inner circle of humanity" are the sustainers of the Earth: by means of the energy produced by the "thirty-six" the Earth remains in its planetary course. This idea was central to the earlier practices of the Oragean Modernists. But the goal seems to have changed, and the Oragean Modernists seem to have gone into their Marxist phase in search of a new type of "food." While at one time the Oragean Modernists directed their efforts toward achieving an elevated minority,—the supermen—an evident shift in the conception of the food that must be supplied to the Moon took place in the 1930s. As I have stated above, the type of food required by the Moon is said to change, but we might wonder how anyone is to determine what comprises the new requirement. The point where this question intrudes marks the limit where esotericism begins to leave the researcher outside. But as Hurston shows through her exaggerated repetition of "mass" (335, 336), the "shrimp" is a new type of food; it is a highly motivated and selfless "mass" movement.

As we have seen, Ellison and Hurston cover the same historical period of time in their novels, and they report on the same events, though in markedly differing styles. Neither account is very clear on its own, but when they are combined they make possible the tracking of the Oragean Modernist intervention in history. While the esotericists themselves have pointed out the parallels to the Christ-drama, only a few points allow any comparison to be made between the events of the past and the present. One point is the instance in which George Schuyler plays the "Judas" role in the Angelo Herndon narrative. Ultimately, Angelo Herndon went into the background, and the Scottsboro Nine became the featured players in the Oragean Modernist's "objective" drama. The Scottsboro Nine were drawn by Aaron Douglas, who rendered them sensitively in pastel in the *Neue Sachlichkeit* (New Objectivity) style. Douglas reverted to an earlier realist style, creating a poignant modern icon in order to more effectively portray the accused rapists as martyrs. Aside from those instances, there are only dim indications of the drama. In one document Melvin Tolson assumed the Judas role in the esoteric Scottsboro Nine drama. Tolson wrote a newspaper column in the Washington Tribune from 1937 to 1944. Tolson's column was written in the esoteric cabala code; on the surface the column was written in a very provocative style. Perhaps this was why Tolson is associated with the function of applying "shocks" in Ellison's presentation of Tolson as the Vet in *Invisible Man.* In his column

"Candid Camera Shots of Negro Intellectuals," June29, 1940, Tolson wrote about an aborted Harlem rally for the Scottsboro Nine that he and Langston Hughes attended in 1932. Tolson's column is set up to be a full, though highly compressed, exposure of the Oragean Moderrnist intervention in history using the Scottsboro Nine. The column is introduced by a "lawful inexactitude" that establishes that the column is filled with esoteric information, that it is a "legominism." Tolson's subtitle, "A Negro Poet and a Taxicab in the rain—1932," provides an incorrect date for the aborted rally. The rally took place on October 21, 1931. In 1932 Hughes was on an extended national poetry tour followed by a long stay in the Soviet Union. This mistake is followed up by an account of some advice given to Hughes by a "lady" in "an elegant sugar Hill parlor." The "lady" tells Hughes how he must dress to appear before "distinguished audiences." As Hughes was to appear before black rural farmers in the South in 1931, the advice is absurd: there were no "distinguished audiences" to be had: the passage is yet another "lawful inexactitude" to reinforce the original absurd thrust. Tolson then goes on to encode the names of A.R. Orage ("elegant parlor), C. Daly King (thus the use of "lady" three times along with "soaking"), P.D. Ouspensky (third paragraph), to refer to the passion ("passionately"), to encode the word "messiah," to present the Judas kiss ("skids"), and to confirm the use of cabala (a taxicab… torrential"). Tolson's assumption of the Judas role is manifest, for he states "But I'm to feel a hundred times that I double-crossed the Scottsboro boys!"

Oragean Modernist literary production did not address the activity of "objective" drama directly through texts that were literary protests. One of the few texts that have been attributed to expressing protest is Arna Bontemps's historical novel, *Black Thunder.* Bontemps published *Black Thunder* in 1936, a novel "inspired and deeply informed by his anguished and brooding response to the Scottsboro case" (Miller 133). Bontemps established believable credentials as a leftist: "He was active in the pro-Communist South Side Writers Club of Chicago, had trusted Communist friends, signed on with activities sponsored by the League of American Writers, and maintained revolutionary convictions and informal links, though not official ties, to the Party" (Washington "Lives"). Scholarly accounts of the Harlem Group list Bontemps as having attended some of Toomer's Gurdjieff meetings in the 1920s, but he is not supposed to have established a serious interest in esotericism. Bontemps's novel of black revolution, *Black Thunder* (1936), is, however, an esoteric text similar in pattern to the earlier novels by Van Vechten, Schuyler, Larsen, Thurman, and Hurston. Bontemps's novel is heavily coded: *Black Thunder*—a poor title for "a story that concluded not with material triumph over racial oppression but with the failure to achieve emancipation" (Leroy-Frazier "Othered")—, phonetically suggests the words "tac[tical] blunder"— as in **Bl**ack *Th***under**— in keeping with the account of the incompetent slave rebellion that it narrates. Like the other Harlem esoteric novels, the text is laced with intentional errors ("lawful inexactitudes"), such as the spelling of "Pharoah" for Pharaoh (Bontemps 69); Pharoah, the pumpkin-colored alleged betrayer of the rebellion is the novel's rendering of Gurdjieff, and he is given the name of an enslaver as befits the Oragean tendency to disparage Gurdjieff. Old Ben (10) is the novel's embodiment of P. D. Ouspensky. Bontemps's novel is dense with the names of the Gurdjieffian teachers coded into the phonetic *cabala* on every page —e.g., A. R. Orage: "hearing…word…large" (66), "cellar and warm porridge" (141), and "mortar trough" (162). *Black Thunder* includes the allegories, concepts, and the vocabulary of Orage's lectures—e.g., "intervals," "work," "shocks," "circles," "force," "observation," and "sleep."

Aaron Douglas taught art at Fisk University in Nashville, Tennessee from 1939 to 1966; Arna Bontemps was the head librarian at Fisk University from 1943 to 1964. Librarian Arna Bontemps acquired Jean Toomer's papers for Fisk University in the 1960s. Melvin Tolson coached the Wiley college debate team so that he could visit esotericists across the country. In a 1939 report he mentioned debates with Fisk University. In 1949 Georgia O'Keefe, a follower of A.R. Orage, donated a portion of her husband's high-profile collection of twentieth-century art to Fisk University. More research is needed to investigate the question of the degree to which the Oragean Modernists were using Fisk University as a headquarters.

To avoid a potential misunderstanding, this point must be made outright and unequivocally: *For the Oragean Modernists the Communist movement was a form of sleep.* If Communism was class war, then as Colin Wilson called it in his study of the Fourth Way, the Oragean Modernists pursued "a war against sleep" [*The War against Sleep: The Philosophy of Gurdjieff*, 1980]. Orage emphasized this point, and it was a fundamental idea that was central to the Oragean Modernist's texts. Gurdjieff made no compromise with sleep:

> Critics note that Gurdjieff gives no value to most of the elements that comprise the life of an average man. According to Gurdjieff, everything an "average man" possesses, accomplishes, does, and feels is completely accidental and without any initiative. A common everyday ordinary man is born a machine and dies a machine without any chance of being anything else. This belief seems to run counter to the Judeo-Christian tradition that man is a living soul. Gurdjieff believed that the possession of a soul (a state of psychological unity which he equated with being "awake") was a "luxury" that a disciple could attain only by the most painstaking work of over a long period of time. The majority—in whom the true meaning of the gospel failed to take root —went the "broad way" that "led to destruction." (Wikipedia "George Gurdjieff)

This point about the "accidental" nature of human life is made over and over in the novels that I have examined in this study. Thus now that we have reached the phase of the "objective" drama in which the Oragean Modernists in some cases have joined the CP (Louise Thompson, Aaron Douglas) or were aligned as "fellow travelers" (Augusta Savage, Dorothy West, Arna Bontemps, John Dos Passos, Dawn Powell, Lincoln Kirstein, James Agee, and Melvin B. Tolson). Similarly, the conservative postures adopted by

Zora Neale Hurston and George Schuyler are merely their roles in the "objective" drama: beyond our being able to see that they have assumed these disguises, we can only guess at their motivations.

As to the matter of how the Oragean Modernists might have evaluated their program, again all that can be said is that an esoteric group keeps its own secrets. If the Oragean Modernists actually saw themselves as the "inner circle of humanity" with the task of saving the Earth from destruction, then since the Earth continues to maintain its orbit through the cosmos, I believe that it is safe to conclude that the followers of Orage must have concluded that their efforts were sufficient. This notion of success is perhaps reified in Hurston's commitment to writing a novel about Herod Antipas. Hurston states in the introduction to her novel about Herod that "If Herod's acts and motivation appear exotic to us of the West in the latter half of the Twentieth Century A.D., we must bear in mind that Herod belonged to, and was a very active participant, in that century of decision which still is influential in our lives at this moment" (Introduction). The implication is that she also lived in a century of decision, and that in writing about Herod's time she was also describing how the "the zig-zag lightning of fate" (Hurston Introduction) had affected her own time. But even as she commences her narrative, Hurston's Introduction situates her novel within an esoteric discourse, for the "zig-zag lightning" that she speaks of is a principle aspect of the Kabbalah:

> The Divine Lightning Bolt is an attempt by God to reconnect with man, after the fall of man, God became disconnected from us and us from God. The Lightning Bolt moves downwards through the Tree-of-life in a zig-zag motion from Kether to Chokhmah back to Binah and down to Malkuth. While man attempts to reconnect with God by moving upward through the Tree, God moves down the tree to meet with us. (Rowlinson "Lightning Bolt")

And if the association is pursued, we can come to the conclusion that while the Jewish mystics picture the lightning descending down the Tree of Life, the same idea in the Gurdjieff Work is also described in *In Search of the Miraculous* in terms of an octave, the Ray of Creation and therefore implicitly in terms of an enneagram. Thus the meaning of Hurston's novel *The Story of Herod the Great* is from its inception mystical, and it testifies to the successful restoration of the planet Earth in the cosmic system by the Oragean Modernists in the 20th century. Shown below is a rendering by Gurdjieff of the Cosmic Octave, his depiction of the "zig-zag lightning" to which Hurston refers in her Introduction to her final novel:

The Cosmic Octave

Conclusion—Oragean Modernism as Psychohistory

An early reader of this study observed that I had brought the narrative to a close without resolving the question of how we are to assess the Oragean Modernists. I had not said anything conclusive about the Oragean Modernist movement in the conviction that to do so would be hasty. Had the scholars and critics of Modernism not passed over occultism, had they situated modern texts in the intellectual context out of which they were conceived, the last seventy-five years would not have been spent pursuing a variety of revisionist controversies over literary theory that had little to do with understanding the literature written in the modern period. It did not seem useful to suppose that the conclusion of my study was the place to try to make up for the neglect caused by so long a period of confusion. But upon reflection, I soon hit upon one notion that might be a useful addition to the opening of the Pandora's Box that allowed the Oragean Modernists to escape.

It came to me to try to put a name to the Oragean Modernist program. Were it possible to position them in accordance with some recognizable narrative, that act might usefully conclude the announcement of their existence. If the question to be addressed is "Were the Oragean Modernists insane," my thought was that this can be put to rest if we take a wide view of the world and look at what passes for sanity. While the Oragean Modernist beliefs seem crazy, they are no crazier than the beliefs of such institutions as the Catholic Church or the Communist Party. Both invest a great deal of energy into supporting outlandish and inevitable futures. In a very real sense, the Oragean Modernist program was simply yet another set of eschatological convictions. Their major difference from these institutional systems of belief is that they were grounded in individual action. Through the embrace of esoteric practices, a small number of individuals took responsibility for the direction of the history of the plane Earth. For the purposes of this discussion, I want to call this behavior the practice of *psychohistory*. I do not really like having to use this term, for it is in danger of derailing my discussion, but I am using it in a provisional manner, and if anything emerges that serves better than *psychohistory*, I will rapidly move to adopt it instead. It seems to me that immediately *psychohistory* causes a problem, as it has since the 1970s come into use to address the entrance of psychoanalysis into the study of history; see "The incommensurability of psychoanalysis and history" by Joan W. Scott. This is not the *psychohistory* of which I want to speak. The psychohistory of which I am thinking does not exist beyond the pages of the science fiction novels of Isaac Asimov (*Foundation*) and Frank Herbert (*Dune*). Both of these writers have invented groups that were capable of analyzing and directing the course of planetary histories. And it was Asimov who first coined the term p*sychohistory* to suit the scientists-conspirators in his novel *Foundation*. As I have already indicated in my study, Frank Herbert's conception of such a group was rooted in esotericism, so Herbert comes much closer to the Oragean Modernists in some ways. Asimov's psychohistorians were technocrats—a much different conception of who would be directing history and how they would be doing it. Asimov's psychohistory is a fictional science in his Foundation universe, which combines history, sociology, etc., and mathematical statistics to make general predictions about the future behavior of very large groups of people, such as the Galactic Empire.

A.R. Orage's psychohistory was based on the practical application of the laws that make up part of the Hidden Learning:

> The Hidden Learning has existed (as it exists today) at all times of which we know, although only seldom appearing upon the surface of what the late M. Ouspensky called Public History or the History of Crime, viz., the history of the school books, which deals with wars, conspiracies, violence and tyrannies. As now and then we catch vague glimpses of the Hidden Learning, it appears in many different guises or versions —the East Indian version of the Baghavad Gita, the medieval rendition of the Orders of Chivalry and of the original Rosy Cross, perhaps in the every earliest of the

Christian and Mohammedan accounts, perhaps also in the initial interpretation of the Lamaists whose descendants still inhabit Thibet, and so on. And once it even appeared with accustomed clarity in Public History itself, in the official religion of Ancient Egypt whose complexities are rendered only the more dubious by the anthropological naiveté of professional Egyptology but which shine with an almost unbelievable illumination when a few key principles of the Hidden Learning have been achieved. (*Oragean Version 4*)

The adherents of the Hidden Learning had erected the Horus-Osiris religion and a subsequent form of that original religion, the Christian religion. Such reformations through the technique of *Objective* Drama, were again called for in the modern period, and like the Pharaonic Egyptians and the Essenes, the Oragean Modernists set about the formulation of a new psychohistoric apparatus that would allow them to introduce the appropriate materials into operation.

It was obvious to anyone with any perception that after the First World War the planet was in crisis. The Oragean Modernists were just one of many groups that were struggling to save the planet. One salient truth directs my evaluation of the Oragean Modernists's program to save the Earth from destruction. While their beliefs may seem absurd, we see that their activities were played out against the panorama of a sleeping humanity. For, whatever else we may say, the central premise of the Gurdjieff Work—that men are asleep—is irrefutable. Given this starting place we must realize that once it has been discovered that humanity is asleep, the awakened people are plunged into a quandary like no other. Sleep had brought mankind near the brink of planetary destruction. Desperate was the word that C. Daly King used to describe the efforts of the Oragean Modernists. The Oragean Modernists sought to turn the Communists to their own purposes, a plan that was hatched primarily out of the notion that revolutionary Communism was nothing but another form of sleep.

While Marxist utopianism is still taken seriously by many American intellectuals, if we are to compare the record of the Communists to the supposed absurdity of the positions of the Oragean Modernists, we have to confront the strange blindness of the Marxists to self-criticism and to self-analysis. Criticism from outside is quick to point out the obvious atrocities committed in the name of Marxist perfectionism. In the introduction to *The Black Book of Communism: Crimes, Terror, Repression* (1997), editor Stéphane Courtois states that "...Communist regimes... turned mass crime into a full-blown system of government." He claims that a death toll totals 94 million. What this says to me s that whatever else one might want to say about Communism, its example shows that man is asleep. If we see the Oragean Modernists in their true context, faced with an historical cascade of mass wars waged with industrial-technological weaponry, totalitarian governments, intellectual and spiritual crises, and economic failures, is there any wonder that these relatively sensitive, intelligent, and desperate people would embrace a teaching that promised to eradicate the problems that the planet faced by placing its fate within their own hands. Instead of struggling against other races and classes— primitive practices of projection and scapegoating that guaranteed the deaths of millions—they strove to resolve Earth's manifold problems by struggling against the source of all of the problems— the cosmic imbalances resulting from the energies that they felt were streaming up to feed the Moon. If nothing else, by choosing the Moon as their enemy they assumed responsibility for the Earth without deeming mass murder a legitimate technique for social improvement. "Sleep" as Gurdjieff defined it is not part of conventional psychology: it cannot be struggled against, since for Freudians it does not exist. The Oragean Modernists were psychohistorians. The very science that argued against esotericism was responsible for the catastrophe of modernity. Science was itself a major form of sleep. Thus by applying psychohistory, the Oragean Modernists were free to construct an entirely new morality, a new epistemology, and a new futurism. Along the way out of their present crisis, they hoped to create a new form of human consciousness and a new relationship between the higher beings of the planetary system.

Endnotes

[1]George I. Gurdjieff was born in the area between Greece and the Caspian Sea in the late 1860s or early 1870s. He grew up in a Christian home (Greek or Russian Orthodox), but, as a child, was exposed to a variety of religious practices by local populations. Aside from such generalizations, nothing about his first forty years that can be corroborated independently from his philosophically instructive autobiography, *Meetings with Remarkable Men* (1963), is available. What is reliably known about Gurdjieff's life dates from the time of his arrival in Moscow at the beginning of the First World War. Two accounts provide parallel chronologies of Gurdjieff's activities during the period 1917-1929. One of these is that of the Russian polymath, P. D. Ouspensky, whose work, *In Search of the Miraculous: Fragments of an Unknown Teaching*, was first published, posthumously, in 1949. The second is that of Thomas and Olga de Hartmann, whose *Our Life with Mr. Gurdjieff*, first published in 1964, was reissued in expanded editions in 1983 and 1992. Gurdjieff was in the Russian cities of Moscow, St. Petersburg, Essentuki, and Tiflis, among others, until 1920, then briefly in Constantinople and Berlin. He arrived in Paris in 1922, where, at first, he rented a house in the Auteuil district that was divided into three flats. Gurdjieff lived on the ground floor, women on the second, men on the third. "Every morning, after breakfast," Butkowsky recalled, "we all went by tram to Jacques Dalcrose's studio, which Gurdjieff had rented, to practice our dancing for several hours. . . . Our evenings were spent with Gurdjieff, listening either to him or to two of his pupils discussing various problems, followed by general questions in which everyone would join." In October 1922 Gurdjieff and his followers moved to Fountainbleau, located south of Paris. In each of these places he put in motion his experimental center for the study of consciousness. Gurdjieff's system of ideas and values was so complex and interconnected that, looking back, it is difficult to select a single aspect or idea as the "basic" one. Common to the several approaches Gurdjieff employed was the principle that his ideas needed to be reinvented, rediscovered, in the experience of

the pupil. For this reason he said, as Ouspensky later put it, that "the study of psychology begins with the study of oneself." Self-study, as pupils were to learn quickly, was never a matter of quiet contemplation in a cell; it was just the opposite. Gurdjieff threw his people into unexpected, often strenuous, activities reminiscent of the style of Marpa, the thirteenth-century Tibetan teacher of Milarepa. The most elaborate of these research centers, called the Institute for the Harmonious Development of Man, was that at Fountainbleau, which operated from 1922 to 1934 on the grounds of a mansion that had belonged to a member of the French aristocracy of the eighteenth century. One of the characteristic activities pursued at these institutes was the study of Gurdjieff's original choreographed dances, which, during the years in Russia, were called "Sacred Gymnastics," and which, after the arrival of Gurdjieff in France, were called "Movements." Financial support for Gurdjieff's activities in Western Europe came initially from England, where his ideas found a receptive audience, and where, from the early 1920s to his death in 1947, Ouspensky made his principal residence. Later, with Gurdjieff's tour of New York and Chicago in 1924, a considerable American following developed, thanks in large measure to the successful efforts of A. R. Orage in attracting American writers and artists. Gurdjieff returned to the United States on several occasions during the periods 1929-35, 1939 and 1948-49. ("Gurdjieff in America: An Overview" George Baker and Walter Driscoll)

[2]Since his revival as a literary artist in the 1960s his supposed rejection of his black identity has come in for a great deal of analysis and discussion. Jean Toomer's status in esoteric circles was just as controversial as his racial status. In 1926 when Toomer assumed direction of esoteric groups in Chicago, Gorham Munson said, "He play acts as a spiritual leader" ("Significance").

[3]Both Stein and Toomer wrote fourth dimensional fiction. Karren Alenier cogently describes Stein's style as follows:

Characteristic of her style is repetition, lack of literary allusion, deceptive simplicity, use of accessible vocabulary, odd juxtapositions of details, suspension of usual logic, contradiction, and words producing a meditative, hypnotic, and harmonic effect on the reader. *One of her goals for her writing was to create the continuous present.* She does this by using "ing" words. Trained as a scientific researcher (she did her undergraduate studies under William James at Harvard/ Radcliffe), her approach to writing is methodical and grounded to things and people most readers would be familiar with. Unlike other writers of her time, her work shows no alienation, no social judgment, no anger, no fear. As a writer Stein never manipulated her reader emotionally. What evolves from the play Stein creates with words is a Cubistic perspective that allows the reader to see more than one facet of an object or person with all its humor, tragedy, and contradictions. (Alenier "Gertrude Stein"; emphasis added)

Similarly, Toomer's novel, *Cane*, invoked "A universe that joins space and time into a continuous flow of "now," in which fragments of past and future are revealed in the present moment" (Kerman 114).

[4]In the Oragean version of the Gurdjieff Work all humans belong to the same category—that of not being men: "For us, *who are not yet men*, that responsibility is but the weightier by reason of the words, not yet.... Every man must somehow find how he can become genuinely human; and to discover this, he must first find out what 'human' really means." (King 222; emphasis added)

[5]"Man number one is the man of the physical body. Man number two is the emotional man. Man number three is the man of reason whose knowledge is based on scholastics. Man number four is a man who has ideals. Man number five is a man who has reached unity and has already been crystallized. Man number six is very

close to the ideal man, but some of his properties have not yet become permanent. Man number seven is the man who had reached the full development possible to man." (Kerr "Notes")

[6]Gurdjieff is often cast in the novels of *esoteric realism* as an extremely disagreeable woman. In Nella Larsen's *Quicksand* the Gurdjieff character is a man who has murdered his wife and having assumed her identity works as a political activist and speaker on women's rights.

[7]In *The Blues Detective* Stephen Soitos has it that a *community* of detectives solves the case. This device allows him to rationalize all of the absurd and disparate elements that signal that the text is esoteric and coded. The murder is committed with a *handkerchief* (a conventional Oragean code for Gurdjieff). Rudolph Fisher was an avowed individualist. The supposition that he installed a community as hero in his novel is testimony to the determination of Soitos to supply Fisher with a set of values that are sanctioned by contemporary Afrocentric thought but have no resonance with the radical elitism of Oragean Modernism.

[8]Oragean Modernism was above the quest for an "objective" literature. The Oragean Modernists were inspired by Gurdjieff's view of the works of "objective" art that had come down to modern man. what follows is the passage from P. D. Ouspensky's *In Search of the Miraculous* (pages 295-297), that presents Gurdjieff's most influential statement on "objective" art. The speaker is Gurdjieff:

> You must first of all remember that there are two kinds of art, one quite different from the other -- objective art and subjective art. All that you know, all that you call art, is subjective art, that is, something that I do not call art at all because it is only objective art that I call art.
> To define what I call objective art is difficult first of all because you ascribe to subjective art the characteristics of objective art, and secondly because

when you happen upon objective works of art you take them as being on the same level as subjective works of art.

I will try to make my idea clear. You say -- an artist creates. I say this only in connection with objective art. In relation to subjective art: that with him 'it is created.' You do not differentiate between these, but this is where the whole difference lies. Further you ascribe to subjective art an invariable action, that is you expect works of subjective art to have the same reaction on everybody. You think, for instance, that a funeral march should provoke in everyone sad and solemn thoughts and that any dance music, a *komarinsky* for instance, will provoke happy thoughts. But in actual fact this is not so at all. Everything depends upon association. If on a day that a great misfortune happens to me I hear some lively tune for the first time this tune will evoke in me sad and oppressive thoughts for my whole life afterwards. And if on a day when I am particularly happy I hear a sad tune, this tune will always evoke happy thoughts. And so with everything else.

The difference between objective art and subjective art is that in objective art the artist really does 'create,' that is he makes what he intended, he puts into his work whatever ideas and feelings he wants to put into it. And the action of this work upon men is absolutely definite; they will, of course each according to his own level, receive the same ideas and the same feelings that the artist wanted to transmit to them. There can be nothing accidental either in the creation or in the impressions of objective art.

In subjective art everything is accidental. The artist, as I have already said, does not create; with him 'it creates itself.' This means that he is in the power of ideas, thoughts, and moods which he himself does not understand and over which he has no control whatever. They rule him and they express themselves in one form or another. And when they have accidentally taken this or that form, this form just as accidentally produces on man this or that action according to his mood, tastes, habits, the nature of the hypnosis under which he lives, and so on. There is nothing invariable; nothing is definite here. In objective art there is nothing indefinite. ... I measure the merit of art by its *consciousness* and you measure it by its *unconsciousness* . We cannot understand one another. A work of objective art ought to be a *book* as you call it; the only difference is that the artist transmits his ideas not directly through words or signs or hieroglyphs, but through certain feelings which he excites consciously and in an orderly way, knowing what he is doing and why he does it. ... principles must be understood. If you grasp the principles you will be able to answer these questions yourselves. But if you do not grasp them nothing that I may say will explain anything to you. It was exactly about this that it was said -- they will see with their eyes and will not perceive, they will hear with their ears and will not understand.

I will cite you one example only -- music. Objective music is all based on *inner octaves.* And it can obtain not only definite psychological results but definite physical results. There can be such music as would freeze water. There can be such music as would kill a man instantaneously. The Biblical legend of the destruction of the walls of Jericho by music is precisely a legend of objective music. Plain music, no matter of what kind, will not destroy walls, but objective music indeed can do so. And not only can it destroy but it can also build up. In the legend of Orpheus there are hints of objective music, for Orpheus used to impart knowledge by music. Snake charmers' music in the East is an approach to objective music, of course very primitive. Very often it is simply one note which is long drawn out, rising and falling only very little; but in this single note 'inner octaves' are going on all the time and melodies of 'inner octaves' which are inaudible to the ears but felt by the emotional center. And the snake hears this music or, more strictly speaking, he feels it, and he obeys it. The same music, only a little more complicated, and men would obey it.

So you see that art is not merely a language but something much bigger. And if you connect what I have just said with what I said earlier about the different levels of man's being, you will understand what is said about art. Mechanical humanity consists of men number one, number two, and number three and they, of course, can have subjective art only. Objective art requires at least flashes of objective consciousness; in order to understand these flashes properly and to make proper use of them a great inner unity is necessary and a great control of oneself.

[9]What Gurdjieff claims that he said to Orage's group is as follows: "Frankly speaking, almost everyone of you gives the impression of, and really is, a man who has all the data to become at any moment a client of one of those, on an American scale, organized houses in New York which are called 'madhouses' and which are supported here by the followers of the English suffragettes" (*Life is Real* 99). See Paul Beekman Taylor's books for another version of these meetings.

Works Cited

Agee, James. *Let's Now Praise Famous Men.* New York: Ballentine, 1939.

Alenier, Karren. "Gertrude Stein." (Web.)

Armstrong, Hamilton Reed. "Modern Art and the Occult." (Web.)

Austgen, Suzanne A. "Agee and Evan's Great Experiment." (Web.)

Baker, George and Walter Driscoll. "Gurdjieff in America: An Overview." (Web.)

Baker, Rob. "No Harem—Gurdjieff and the Women of The Rope." *Gurdjieff International Review.* Web.

Barnes, Djuna. *Nightwood.* (1937) New York: New Directions, 1961.

Bellman "Spectacular Shadows." (Web.)

Benedicto, K. "Food, Secrets, Inclusion." Web.

Benjamin, Harry. *Gurdjieff's System of Human Development: "The Work."* (being a summary of "Basic Self-Knowledge"). New York: Weiser, 1971.

Bennett, John. *Gurdjieff Today.* Charles Town, WV: Claymont Communications, 1978. Web.

Birney, Alice L. "Hurston and Her Plays." (Web.)

Bloom, Harold. *Zora Neale Hurston.* Boston: Chelsea House, 2003.

Bloomberg, Kristen M. Mapel. *Tracing Arachne's Web: Myth and Feminist Fiction.* Gainesville: University of Florida Press, 2001.

Carew, Joy G. *Blacks, Reds, and Russians: Sojourners in Search of the Soviet Promise.* Kindle Edition, 2008.

Carpenter, Humphrey. *The Brideshead Generation: Evelyn Waugh and His Friends.* Boston: Houghton Mifflin, 1990.

Coogle, Matt. "The Historical Significance of *Let Us Now Praise Famous Men.*" (Web.)

Crunden, Robert M. *Body and Soul: the Making of American Modernism: Art, Music and Letters in the Jazz Age 1919-1926.* New York; Basic Books, 2008. (2000). (Web.)

Driscol, J. Walter. "The Essence of Orage: Some Aphorisms and Observations." *Gurdjieff International Review.* (Web.)

Dwight, Jessie. "Gurdjieff Poem." (Web.)

El-Hai, Jack. "Reel Life." Web.

Ellison, Ralph. *Invisible Man.* Kindle Edition, 1952. [New York: Vintage, 1972].

Eppard, Philip B. "Julian English Outside of Samarra." Colby Quarterly. Volume 32.3. 9-1-1996,190-95. Web.

"Extravagant Crowd: Carl Van Vechten's Portraits of Women." The Beinecke Rare Book & Manuscript Library. Web.

Finch, Charles S. *Nile Genesis: An Introduction to the Opus of Gerald Massey.* 2006. Web.

Finch, Henry Leroy. "The Sacred Cosmos: Teachings of G.I. Gurdjieff" in Jacob Needleman and George Baker, eds.*Gurdjieff: Essays and Reflections on the Man and His Teaching* (New York: Continuum, 1996), p. 23.) Web.

Fishburn, Katherine. "Science Fiction or Psycho-Drama?" *Science Fiction Studies.* Vol. 15, No. 1 (Mar., 1988), pp. 48-60. (Web.)

Foley, Barbara. *Wrestling with the Left: The Making of Ralph Ellison's Invisible Man.* Kindle Edition, 2010.

Foster, Don. "The Alchemy Academic Forum." 201-250. (Web.)

"Fourth Way." (Web.)

Genette, Gerard. *Fiction and Diction.* Ithaca: Cornell UP, 1991.

"George Gurdjieff." Wikipedia.

Gibbons, Tom H. 1973. *Rooms in the Darwin Hotel: studies in English literary criticism and ideas, 1880-1920.* Nedlans, WA: University of Western Australia Press.

Gilkyson, Walter. "A Prisoner of Memory." *Harper's Magazine.* V. 161. November 1930, 651-664.

_____. *The Lost Adventurer.* New York: Scribner's, 1927.

Ginsburg, Seymor B. "Gurdjieff Unveiled." (Web.)

Glenn, Isa. *East of Eden.* Garden City, N. Y.: Doubleday, Doran and Company, Inc., 1932.

Griffiths, Frederick T. "Ralph Ellison, Richard Wright, and the Case of Angelo Herndon," *African American Review* 35, no. 4 (2000), 615–37.

Gurdjieff, G.I. *Life is real only then, when "I am".* (Web.)

Harvat, Arvan. "Gurdjieff, Enneagram, and the Fourth Way." (Web.)

Herndon, Angelo. *Let Me Live.* New York: Random House, 1937. Web.

Hocutt, Daniel L. "Richmond-in-Virginia" in the Literary World: Correspondence Between Ellen Glasgow and Carl Van Vechten." (Web.)

Hodd, Tom. *"Literary Modernism and Occult Scholarship: The Rising Academic Tide." The Antigonish Review.* (Web.)

Hume, Elizabeth. "Metathesis." (Web.)

Hurston, Zora Neale. "The Characteristics of Negro Expression." (1934). In *Sweat.* Ed. Cheryl Wall. New Brunswick: Rutgers UP, 1997. 55-71. (Web.)

_____. [Introduction.] "From Herod the Great." *Callaloo.* 34:1, 21-25.

_____. *Seraph on the Suwanee.* New York: Charles Scribner's Sons, 1948.

_____. *Mules and Men.* Web.

_____. *Moses, Man of the Mountain.* Lippincott, 1939, reprinted, University of Illinois Press, 1984.

Kellner, Bruce. *Carl Van Vechten and the Irreverent Decades,* University of Oklahoma Press, 1968.

Kenyon, Bernice Lesbia. *The Harpers Monthly.* November 1936, 587-597.

Kerman, Cynthia Earl and Richard Eldridge. 1987. *The Lives of Jean Toomer: A Hunger for Wholeness.* Baton Rouge: Louisiana State University Press.

Kerr, David. "Similarities Between the Philosophies of George Ohsawa and George Gurdjieff: Notes." (Web.).

King, C. Daly. 1951. *The Oragean Version.* Unpublished. (Web.).

Kirschke, Amy Helene. *Aaron Douglas: Art, Race, & the Harlem Renaissance.* Jackson: University Press of Mississippi, 1995.

Kirstein, Lincoln. (Web.)

Lackey, Michael. "Zora Neale Hurston's 'Herod the Great': (Web.)" *Callaloo* 34.1 (1/1/2011), 100-20.

Langdon, Kevin. "Gurdjief's Ideas about Man and the Universe." 1986. Web.

Leroy-Frazier, Jill. 2010. "Othered Southern Modernism: Arna Bontemps's *Black Thunder. Mississippi Quarterly.* 63:1-2. (Web.).

Ludington, Townsend. "John Dos Passos, 1896-1970: Modernist Recorder of the American Scene." *Virginia Quarterly Review.* Autumn 1996, 565-580. Web.

MacFarlane, Ian C. "Gurdjieff's Cosmology." *The Endless Search.* (Web.)

McKeon, Michael, ed. *Theory of the Novel: A Historical Approach.* Baltimore: Johns Hopkins University Press, 2000.

Markowitz, Norman. "Telling It From the Mountain Top." Communist Party USA, 2004. (Web.))

Marshall, Taylor. "Baptism By Blood and the Apostle James." (Web.)

Massey Gerald. *Ancient Egypt; The Light of the World.* Web.

Mills, A.D. [2003]. (Web.).

Miller, James A. *Remembering Scottsboro: The Legacy of an Infamous Trial.* Princeton: Princeton University Press, 2009.

Mistlberger, P. T. *The Three Dangerous Magi: Osho, Gurdjieff, Crowley.* Axis Mundi Books (November 16, 2010)

Munson, Gorham. "Orage in America." (Web.)

Needleman, Jacob. "G. I. Gurdjieff and His School." *Gurdjieff International Review.* Web.

O'Hara, John. *Appointment in Samarra.* New York: Random House, 2009. (1934).

Oderberg I. M. "H. P. Blavatsky's Cultural Impact." (Web.)

Orage, A.R. "Are We Awake?" (1925). *Gurdjieff International Review.* Web.

Ouspensky, P.D. *In Search of the Miraculous: Fragments of an Unknown Teaching.* New York: Harcourt, Brace, 1949. Web. (Web.).

Owens, Terry Winter and Suzanne D. Smith. "Commentary" [on *All and Everything: Beelzebub's Tales To His Grandson*]. (Web.)

Panek, LeRoy. *Reading Early Hammet.* Jefferson, NC: McFarland, 2004.

Patterson, William Patrick. "The Last Esoteric Message." The Gurdjieff Legacy Foundation. Web.

Post, Charlie. "The Comintern." (Web.)

Powell, Dawn. *The Locusts Have No King.* New York: Yarrow Press, 1990.

_____. *Turn, Magic Wheel.* New York: Farrar & Rinehart, 1936. Kindle edition.

Rauve, Rebecca. "An Intersection of Interests: Gurdjieff's Rope Group as a Site of Literary Production." *Twentieth Century Literature* Vol. 49, No. 1, American Writers and France (Spring, 2003), 46-81].

Rawlings, Marjorie Kinnan. *South Moon Under.* Gutenberg Project. Web.

_____. *The Yearling.* Gutenberg Project. Web.

Rieger, Christopher B. *Clear-Cutting Eden: Representations of Nature in Southern Fiction, 1930-1950.* Dissertation, Louisiana SU, 2002. Web.

Rowlinson, Patrick. "The Divine Lightning Bolt." (Web.)

Schneider, Frederick. "A Passion for Understanding." [Edited with commentary by Allan Lindh]. 1923-27. Web.

Shirley, John. "What If It's True?: The Terror of the Situation." *John Shirley Blog.* Web.

Soitos, Stephen. *The Blues Detective: A Study of African American Detective Fiction.* Amherst: University of Massachusetts Press, 1996.

Staley, D."Negative Effects." *Gurdjieff and the Fourth Way: A Critical Appraisal.* (Web.)

Stone, Dan. 2002. *Breeding Superman: Nietzsche, Race and Eugenics in Edwardian and Interwar Britain.* (Studies in Social and Political Thought.) Liverpool: Liverpool University Press.

Taylor, Paul Beekman. 2001.*Gurdjieff and Orage: Brothers in Elysium.* York Beach: Weiser Books.

_____. *Gurdjieff's America: Mediating the Miraculous.* Cambridge, UK:Lighthouse Editions, 2004.

Thurman, Wallace. *Infants of the Spring.* New York: Macaulay Co., 1932.

Tolson, Melvin B. "The Man from Halicarnassus." *Poetry.* LXXXI.1 (October, 1952), 75-77.

_____. *Libretto for the Republic of Liberia..* New York: Twayne, 1953.

_____. "E. & O. E." *"Harlem Gallery and Other Poems of Melvin B. Tolson."* Edited by Raymond Nelson. Charlottesville: University Press of Virginia, 1999.

_____. *Harlem Gallery: Book 1, The Curator.* With an introd. by Karl Shapiro. New York: Twayne, 1965.

_____. *Caviar and Cabbage: Selected Columns by Melvin B. Tolson from the Washington Tribune, 1937-1944,* ed. Robert M. Farnsworth (Columbia: U Missouri P,1982), 106.

Two Rivers Farm. "The Work." (Web.)

Van Vechten,Carl. *Firecrackers. A Realistic Novel.* New York: Knopf, 1925.

_____. *Nigger Heaven.* New York: Knopf, 1926.

Vincenti, Marissa. "A MATTER OF SPIRIT AARON DOUGLAS, GURDJIEFFIAN THOUGHT, AND THE EXPRESSION OF 'CONSCIOUS ART.'"*International Review of African American Art.* 21 no3. 11-15, 2007. Web.

Wall, Cheryl A. "Zora Neale Hurston's Essays: On Art and Such" (Web.)

Washington, Mary Helen. "Lives of the Exiles." (review of *The Forging of the Mid-Twentieth-Century Literary Left* by Alan Wald (Chapel Hill: University of North Carolina Press, 2002). *Solidarity.* 2002. Web.

Wellbeloved, Sophia. *Gurdjieff: The Key Concepts.* London and New York: Routledge, 2003.

West, Dorothy. "Room in Red Square." "Challenge": Vol. I, No. 1 (March 1934), 10-15.

West, Nathaniel. *Miss Lonelyhearts.* Gutenberg Project. Web. (1933).

Woodruff, Frederick. [Cover]" (Web.)

Woodson, Jon. *To Make a New Race: Gurdjieff, Toomer, and the Harlem Renaissance.* Jackson: UP of Mississippi, 1999.

Young, Judith S. [Department of Astronomy at the University of Massachusetts, Amherst]. "Letter to Jon Woodson." 2 21 2013.

Zimmerman, Patrick. "The Self-Dissatisfied Life and Art of James Agee" (Web.)

Index

Made in United States
North Haven, CT
11 February 2024

48630946R10129